The Railway through Summer Wine Country
Huddersfield - Penistone - Barnsley - Sheffield
Contents

385.094281
HAI

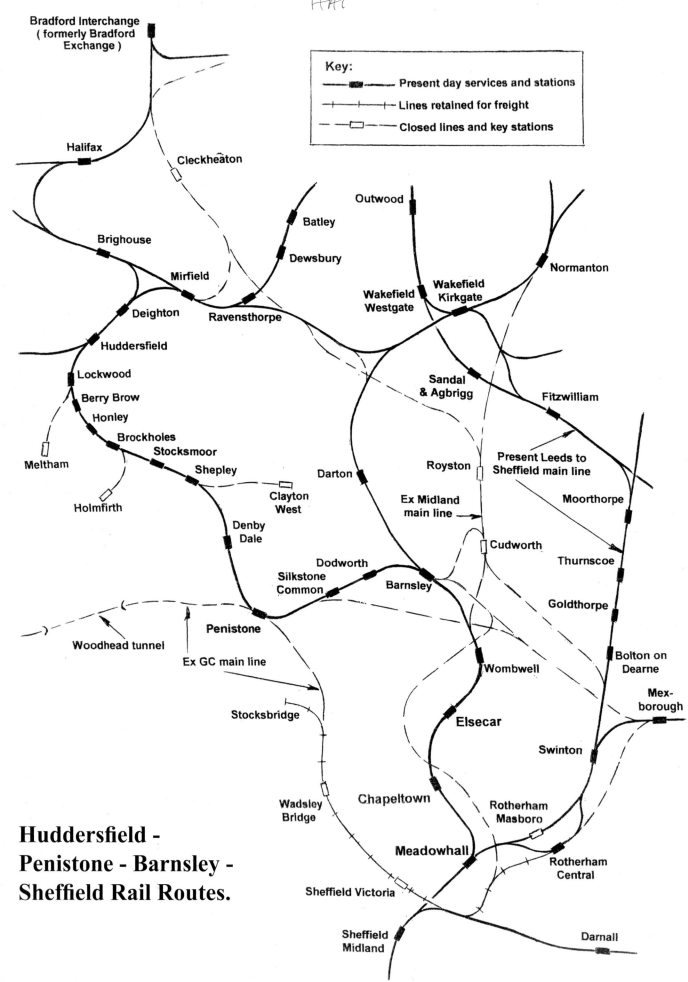

Bradford Interchange
(formerly Bradford
Exchange)

Key:
- Present day services and stations
- Lines retained for freight
- Closed lines and key stations

Halifax

Cleckheaton

Batley

Dewsbury

Outwood

Brighouse

Mirfield

Normanton

Deighton

Ravensthorpe

Wakefield
Westgate

Wakefield
Kirkgate

Huddersfield

Lockwood

Berry Brow

Honley

Sandal
& Agbrigg

Fitzwilliam

Brockholes

Stocksmoor

Meltham

Shepley

Darton

Royston

Present Leeds to
Sheffield main line

Holmfirth

Clayton
West

Ex Midland
main line

Cudworth

Moorthorpe

Denby
Dale

Dodworth

Silkstone
Common

Barnsley

Thurnscoe

Goldthorpe

Penistone

Woodhead tunnel

Ex GC main line

Wombwell

Bolton on
Dearne

Mex-
borough

Stocksbridge

Elsecar

Swinton

Chapeltown

Rotherham
Masboro

Wadsley
Bridge

Meadowhall

Rotherham
Central

Sheffield Victoria

Sheffield
Midland

Darnall

Huddersfield -
Penistone - Barnsley -
Sheffield Rail Routes.

1. Introduction

The popular long running classic BBC television programme 'Last of the Summer Wine' was set and filmed in the Holme valley south of Huddersfield. The series ran from 1973 to 2010 and although centred on the small pennine town of Holmfirth it's success popularised the whole area which has become known as 'Summer Wine' country. This label has been used unofficially to promote the Penistone railway line which serves this rural area as well as connecting the urban centres of West and South Yorkshire. 'Summer Wine' is indeed a very appropriate name to describe the spectacular pennine scenery. Even the old coalfield areas to the south have been very successfully landscaped to make this a very green and picturesque railway..

This book looks at the history and present day evolution of the railways between Huddersfield and Sheffield concentrating on the core route but also including some key associated railways such as the Midland main line, the ex Great Central Woodhead route and developments in the Sheffield and Rotherham areas.

The history of this railway is quite unique. It emerged through the chance joining together of a number of local lines which survived many attempts at closure. Originally steam operated part was electrified then de-electrified to be replaced by diesels The line was originally a main line but rationalisation reduced it to a mostly single track rural backwater before a revival resulted in development with new stations as well as being considered for conversion into a tramway. The present route starts off running on ex Lancashire & Yorkshire Railway tracks to Penistone then using ex Great Central Railway metals to Barnsley before completing the line on the ex Midland route to Sheffield.

My first experience of the Penistone line dates back to 1954 when I visited the town to see the new electric freight locomotives which, with great ease, conveyed the many coal trains which crossed the Pennines to Lancashire and returned with empties. Nothing as modern as this had been seen before in this region. There were many other visits and this railway became one of my all time favourites.

Luckily the line won a reprieve from the Beeching axe but further major changes were ahead with extension of the service to Sheffield, more attempts at closure and eventual savour by the trains being diverted via Barnsley. I was an objector to the later withdrawal of service notices and helped the campaign to save the line. Closure very nearly did happen and it was a very close run thing that the service survived.

Today's route is 37 miles long and traverses the Pennine hills which gives it many very heavy civil engineering features. Between Huddersfield and Barnsley there are major viaducts at Paddock, Lockwood, Denby Dale and Penistone with tunnels at Lockwood, Robin Hood, Thurstonland, Cumberworth, Wellhouse and Oxspring. Because of the high cost of maintenance the line was always an easy target for closure but coal traffic to the many local collieries helped keep the route open for many years. However the route is operated very economically using modern colour light signalling controlled from three signal boxes and in recent times the line has become exclusively for passenger traffic which has grown rapidly with the trains now booming and carrying over 1 million passengers per year.

The Huddersfield to Sheffield service was only saved from closure at the last moment by diversion via Barnsley in 1983. Here a Sheffield bound train on the new route crosses the M1 motorway near Dodworth. Note the scarcity of traffic on the motorway. The track between Penistone and Barnsley had been kept in use after closure to local passenger trains in 1959. A few express trains used it in the 1960's but after this was retained for coal trains.

2. Outline History.

The first trans pennine railway was opened in 1840 by the Manchester & Leeds company, which changed it's name to the Lancashire & Yorkshire Railway in 1847, on a circuitous Calder Valley route via Hebden Bridge, Wakefield and Normanton missing out the major centres of Halifax, Bradford and Huddersfield. Two separate local companies the Leeds, Dewsbury and Manchester Railway and the Huddersfield & Manchester Railway were formed so that by 1848 Huddersfield was served by a direct Manchester to Leeds service with the London & North Western Railway absorbing both companies just before the opening of the new trans-pennine route.

The Huddersfield & Sheffield Junction Railway opened the railway from Huddersfield to Penistone with a branch to Holmfirth in 1850. This company was taken over by the Lancashire & Yorkshire Railway who later opened further branches to Meltham in 1869 and to Clayton West in 1879.

Another company to become part of the Lancashire & Yorkshire was the Sheffield, Rotherham, Barnsley, Wakefield, Huddersfield & Goole Railway which opened a line from the Manchester & Leeds line at Horbury Junction to Barnsley Regent Street later to become Barnsley Exchange.

Further south the Sheffield & Rotherham Railway was opened in 1838 while the North Midland main line from Derby to Leeds began operating in 1840 serving Rotherham Masborough and a Barnsley station located at Cudworth but bypassing Sheffield. These companies became part of the Midland Railway who in 1870 completed a loop line from Chesterfield to Rotherham through Sheffield which included the opening of Midland station and at the same time provided a new line from Cudworth to Barnsley Court House.

The Sheffield, Ashton-under-Lyne and Manchester Railway opened the Woodhead route in 1845 using a station at Sheffield Bridghouses until the opening of Sheffield Victoria station in 1851. This company amalgamated with the Sheffield & Lincolnshire Junction Railway and Great Grimsby & Sheffield Junction Railway to become the Manchester, Sheffield & Lincolnshire from 1847 and later became the Great Central Railway in 1897 when the extension to London was being planned. This company took over the South Yorkshire Railway in 1874 which had opened the Mexborough to Barnsley line in 1851 and completed Penistone to Barnsley in 1859.

The Great Central and Midland Railways competed for passengers on duplicate parallel routes between Sheffield and Barnsley. Trains between Sheffield Victoria and Barnsley Court House began to operate in 1864 but it was 1897 before the start of the Midland Railway train service from Sheffield Midland to Barnsley Court House via Chapeltown.

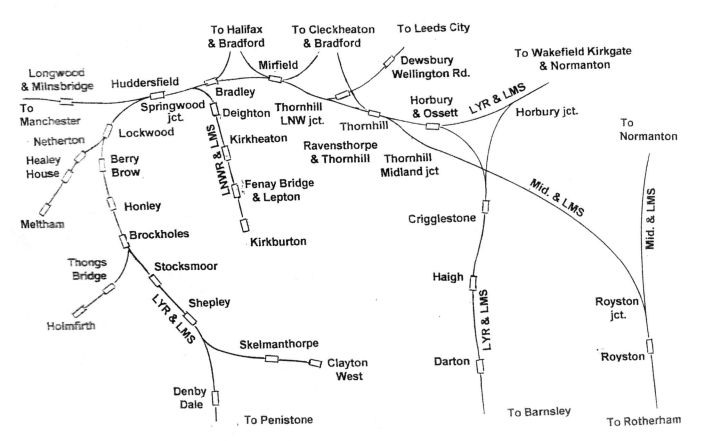

Huddersfield passenger rail routes

Penistone - Barnsley - Rotherham - Sheffield
Passenger Rail Routes.
Hull & Barnsley and some mineral lines omitted for clarity

3. Pre-grouping train services.

Prior to the groupings services were operated by three railway companies, The Midland, Great Central and Lancashire & Yorkshire (this absorbed into the London & North Western Railway in 1921). The Great Central ran an express service from Bradford Exchange departing at 9.55 and 16.55 to London Marylebone via Huddersfield, Penistone and Sheffield Victoria with return services from London at 10.00 and 18.20. In addition there were through London coaches on a train to Sheffield from Halifax (dep. 7.45) and Huddersfield (dep.8.15) All the other local trains on this line terminated at Penistone with connections to Sheffield into GCR Manchester - Sheffield - London main line trains.

The Great Central also ran a daily through coach to London attached to an express at Sheffield Victoria. On the other hand the Midland Railway operated shuttle Barnsley Court House to Cudworth trains to connect with express trains on the Midland main line.

The LYR ran an intense suburban service on the Penistone line with no less than 47 trains in each direction between Huddersfield and Lockwood.

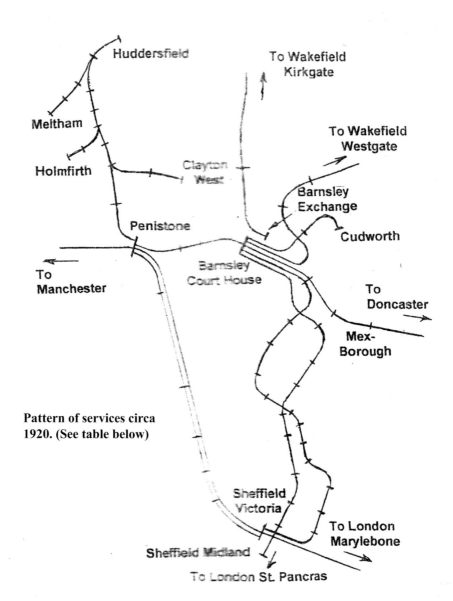

Pattern of services circa 1920. (See table below)

Service operated	Railway Company	Number of daily trains (one way)
Manchester - Penistone - Sheffield Victoria (express)	GCR	15
(Manchester) - Penistone - Sheffield Victoria (local)		10 (a)
Penistone - Barnsley Court House - Doncaster	GCR	10
Barnsley Court House - Leeds Central via Nostell	GCR	5 + 1 (SO)
Barnsley Court House - Sheffield Victoria.	GCR	8
Barnsley Court House - Sheffield Midland	MR	11 + 1 (SO)
Barnsley Court House - Cudworth	MR	21
Wakefield Kirkgate - Barnsley Exchange	LYR	15 (b)
Huddersfield - Meltham	LYR	11 + 1 (SO)
- Holmfirth		17 + 2 (SO)
- Clayton West		9 + 1 (SO)
- Penistone		10 (c)
Total number of trains		142 + 6 (SO)

Notes: (a) 6 of these trains ran Penistone - Sheffield only. (b) Includes one train Leeds Central to Barnsley via Dewsbury and Horbury & Ossett. (c) includes one express Halifax to Sheffield train, other trains terminate at Penistone. SO = Saturdays only.

Sheffield Victoria in pre-grouping days. (Lens of Sutton Association)

Sheffield. Interior of the new Midland Station. "Scott" Series Nr. 644

Sheffield Midland station in 1912 (Lens of Sutton Association)

4. Between the wars

At the start of World War 1 the local railway network had reached it's maximum size and came under Government control for the duration of the war. The system came under great strain in meeting the wartime demands made upon it and with peacetime emerged in rundown condition to a changed world. The result was the grouping of the numerous railway companies into four major railways which became effective from January 1923. Of the area under consideration the Great Central, North Eastern and Hull & Barnsley railways became part of the LNER while the LMS included the takeover of the Midland, London North Western and Lancashire & Yorkshire companies..

The slump in the 1930's followed by a further war had an adverse effect upon railway finances as did the advent of the motor car and motor bus which with steadily improving roads provided growing competition for the railways. This resulted in a loss of passengers from which some lines and many stations never fully recovered. As a result the LNER closed Attercliffe station to passengers in 1927, Staincross and Notton & Royston in 1930 with withdrawal of the Barnsley to Leeds service via Nostell. Similarly the LMS closed Monk Bretton in 1937. Neepsend was permanently closed to passengers by the LNER during World War 2 in 1940.

The Sheffield to Manchester electrification was first proposed by the LNER in 1926 but it was over ten years later before work started in 1936. However this was stopped with the outbreak of war in 1939 until it was completed after the war by British Railways.

Inter War years
LMS locomotive number 10713 heads an LMS train for Huddersfield at Penistone in 1934. The locomotive is an ex LYR 2-4-2 tank type of engine introduced by Aspinall in 1889. Photo: Transport Treasury.

Inter War Years Locomotives.

Most express trains in the Sheffield area were hauled by either 4-4-0 or 4-6-0 locomotives. Gresley in 1928 introduced the Class D49 and here number 359 'The Fitzwilliam' makes a rare appearance at Sheffield Victoria in 1935. Picture: Transport Treasury.

Less common locomotives were the Atlantic type of 4-4-2. Here Robinson Atlantic Class C4 number 5266 at Sheffield Victoria in 1935. These were introduced in 1903 as compound locomotives but the simple 4-6-0 was to find favour as the locomotive to be built in larger numbers. Picture: Transport Treasury.

LNER Class C1 locomotive number 4428 on a passenger train at Sheffield Victoria. Displaced from East Coast express work by Pacifics during the 1930's, the class had several workings to Sheffield from Doncaster; an area traditionally dominated by ex-GCR engines.
Photo: Stephenson Locomotive Society.

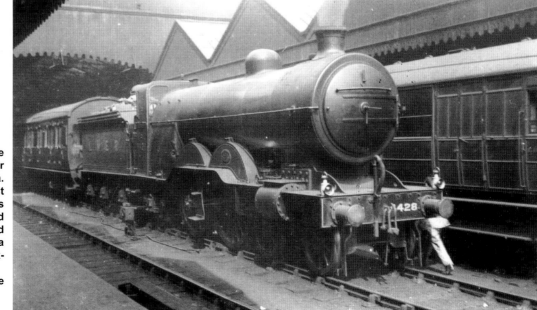

Penistone - Woodhead 1934.

An LNER 4-6-0 Class B17 4-6-0 locomotive No. 2842 'Kilverstone Hall' approaches Penistone station in 1934 with a Manchester to Sheffield train.   Picture: Transport Treasury.

LNER 2-6-0 Class K2 locomotive No. 4636 leaves one of the original Woodhead tunnels with an express train in 1934.   A new double bore tunnel was constructed for the opening of electrified services in 1954. Picture: Transport Treasury.

5. Train services 1947

Train services just after the war had not changed appreciably since pre grouping days. The Barnsley Court House service to Leeds via Nostell had been withdrawn and the LNER service from Barnsley to Sheffield Victoria had become peak hours only but otherwise a daylong service was offered on other lines. The number of stations had reduced to 49.

Rationalisation in the area turned out to be very drastic after an early casualty when the Meltham branch closed in 1949. The duplicate ex - GC Barnsley to Sheffield Victoria service was withdrawn in 1953 The push and pull service from Barnsley to Cudworth ceased to run in 1958 but the following year saw the most reductions with Sheffield Victoria - Penistone local trains, the Penistone - Doncaster

Service operated	Railway	Number of daily trains (one way)
Manchester - Penistone - Sheffield Victoria (express)	LNER	13 + 1 (SO)
(Manchester) - Penistone - Sheffield Victoria (local)		8 (a)
Penistone - Barnsley Court House - Doncaster	LNER	6 + 2 (SO)
Barnsley Court House - Sheffield Victoria.	LNER	3
Barnsley Court House - Sheffield Midland	LMS	8 + 1 (SO)
Barnsley Court House - Cudworth	LMS	16
Wakefield Kirkgate - Barnsley Exchange	LMS	8 + 3 (SO)
Huddersfield - Meltham	LMS	11 + 1 (SO)
- Holmfirth		17 + 2 (SO)
- Clayton West		9 + 1 (SO)
- Penistone		10
Total number of trains		**109 + 11 (SO)**

Long distance services were roughly comparable. The 1947 ABC Rail Guide listed three different ways of travelling between Barnsley and London. To St. Pancras by changing at Cudworth, to Marylebone by changing at Penistone and to Kings Cross by changing at Doncaster.

6. Nationalisation 1948

The railways were in a bad way after serving the country well during the second world war leaving them in a run-down condition requiring major investment. The Government response was the Transport Act of 1947 which nationalised the railway companies to become British Railways from January 1948. The effect of this was rationalisation of routes and modernisation of ageing equipment.

service and Holmfirth branch all curtailed. In the first 10 years of British Railways 25 local stations were closed down.

In 1952 a trial of an ex-GWR diesel railcar in the West Riding led to an order for the introduction of the first BR DMU's in 1954 between Leeds - Bradford / Harrogate. This was followed by the 1955 Modernisation Plan to replace steam with diesel and electric traction. DMU's were introduced between Leeds to Barnsley Exchange in 1958 followed by Sheffield Midland to Barnsley and York while Bradford Exchange - Huddersfield - Clayton West / Penistone DMU's started in 1959. A year later the Barnsley DMU's were linked up to form a new through Leeds - Sheffield local service via Barnsley using an enlarged Exchange station with the Court House station closed along with major route rationalisation.

Barnsley had a suburban station on the Penistone line at Summer Lane until closed in 1959. A view looking towards Penistone in 1956. Photo: StationsUK

Local Trains.

Ex Midland Railway Class 1P 0-4-4T locomotive number 58066 forms the auto train for Barnsley Court House at Cudworth station in 1951. This train formed a push - pull shuttle service from Barnsley to connect with Midland main line trains. The locomotive is in the first plain British Railways livery.
Photo. Initial Photographs / BWLB

The LMS and British Railways also ran a local service on the Midland Main line until withdrawn in 1968. Here ex Midland Railway 4-4-0 Class 4P compound locomotive number 41154 at Cudworth with the 16.10 Leeds to Sheffield stopper in 1951.
Photo: BWLB / Initial Photographics.

The GCR ran local services from Sheffield Victoria to Penistone and Barnsley Court House. Also trains from Penistone to Doncaster via Barnsley. Shown here is the latter service on it's last day before withdrawal. Ex LNER C14 4-4-2 tank number 67445 running bunker first carries notice of cessation of the Penistone - Doncaster passenger service RIP at Wath Central on the last day of operation in 1959.

Local Trains.

The route of the present Huddersfield to Sheffield service emerged by chance as a result of political responses to efforts by British Railways to close passenger services. Previously these trains were provided by three separate services. Here ex LMS Fairburn 2-6-4 tank no. 42152 arrives at Penistone station in 1953 with the 14.55 from Bradford Exchange.
Photo: Initial Photographics.

Ex GC Class J11 0-6-0 freight locomotive number 64398 forms the 17.15 train for Barnsley Court House at Penistone station in 1953.
Photo. Initial Photographs / RJB

Ex GCR tank no. 67445 waits at Sheffield Midland in 1959 with the 12.15 for Barnsley Court House.
Photo: Initial Photographics.

7. Beeching

There were then no further closures until the Beeching Report, called 'The Reshaping of British Railways' was published in 1963 and in an effort to make the railways pay this advocated the withdrawal of passenger services from 5,000 route miles of railway and the closure of 2,363 stations nationally.. The report was a blow to the Penistone line which was proposed for total closure but generally South Yorkshire did not seem to have been hit as hard but this was only because so many local services had already been closed. The Sheffield to Manchester electric trains were not mentioned in the report and so it was assumed that these would continue. The proposals effecting services in the area were:

Passenger Services to be withdrawn.
Huddersfield - Clayton West / Penistone.
Bradford Exchange - Cleckheaton - Mirfield - Huddersfield.
Bradford Exchange - Halifax - Huddersfield.
Leeds City - Cudworth - Sheffield Midland (local).
York - Sheffield Victoria - Nottingham
(GC main line)

Other stations to be closed.
Crigglestone, Cudworth, Darfield, Haigh, Royston and Wath (North)

8. Beeching part 2.

This was published in 1965 and entitled 'The Development of the Major Railway Trunk Routes' looked at duplicate main lines. This saw a future for the Woodhead route but mainly for freight traffic. Later consideration was being given to concentrating Inter city passenger services between Sheffield and Manchester on the Hope Valley route which put a question mark against the electric service via Penistone. The Eastern Region had indicated it's intention to close Sheffield Victoria station and with a new curve at Nunnery services from the east had already been diverted into Sheffield Midland station. This left Victoria station only used by Manchester electric services.

The Minister of Transport had refused British Railway's plans to close the Huddersfield - Penistone / Clayton West services on the grounds that it would cause hardship for passengers. BR's other plan was that Sheffield Victoria station should be closed but this was held up by the Minister of Transport's insistence that having refused closure of the Huddersfield to Penistone trains then BR must maintain a service between Penistone and Sheffield. This was resolved on 5th. January 1970 when the Manchester to Sheffield electric service was withdrawn with the Hudderfield to Penistone diesel service extended to Sheffield Midland with reversal at Woodburn junction.

PAYTRAIN GUIDE
Huddersfield - Sheffield
1 May 1972 to 5 May 1973

PAYTRAIN GUIDE
Leeds - Barnsley - Sheffield
1 May 1972 to 6 May 1973

Paytrains and the Destaffing of stations.

From 1961 economy measures led to staff being withdrawn from stations. The Penistone line led the country with station staff withdrawn and tickets issued on the train. These were then marketed as Paytrains. This started with the Penistone line but was later extended to the Leeds - Barnsley - Sheffield DMU service. Early ticket issuing machines were limited and tickets could only be issued for the branch service with passengers having to rebook at Sheffield or Huddersfield for onward travel. However with better machines passengers can now book to any other station on the national network.

9. The aftermath of Beeching

South Yorkshire handled vast amounts of freight tonnage mainly of coal and steel. One reason for the closure of passenger services was to concentrate resources and investment in freight. The Beeching Report advocated the development of key freight services and the result was the rationalisation and modernisation of freight facilities in the Sheffield area. Main changes were:

New Marshalling Yard and Diesel Depot at Tinsley.
New scissors junction at Aldwarke.
New Sheffield Freight terminal.
New curve at Nunnery.
New NE, NW and SW Tinsley curves.

The 1968 Transport Act allowed Government Grant Aid to be paid to support un-remunerative but socially necessary local rail services. Figures for local trains for 1969 and 1970 were as follows:

Route	1969	1970
Huddersfield - Clayton West / Penistone	£176,000	£130,000
Penistone - Sheffield	£64,000	£44,000
Leeds - Barnsley - Sheffield	£402,000	£245,000

In 1974 Passenger Transport Executives for West and South Yorkshire (WYPTE and SYPTE) were formed. These were controlled by West and South Yorkshire County Council's respectively and would take financial control for local rail services within their county. This was to be done through a Section 20 agreement and it was expected that BR would not continue to run local services within PTE areas which did not have such an agreement.

Therefore by the 1980's with the decline of the basic local industries of coal and steel and more secure passenger services the situation had reversed. Investment had now switched to improving passenger services with the help of local Transport Authorities and money from the European Union. .Closures then concentrated on removing freight capacity with the main casualty being the electric trans-Pennine Woodhead route. However one area of concern was the cost of keeping the Sheffield to Penistone trains running.

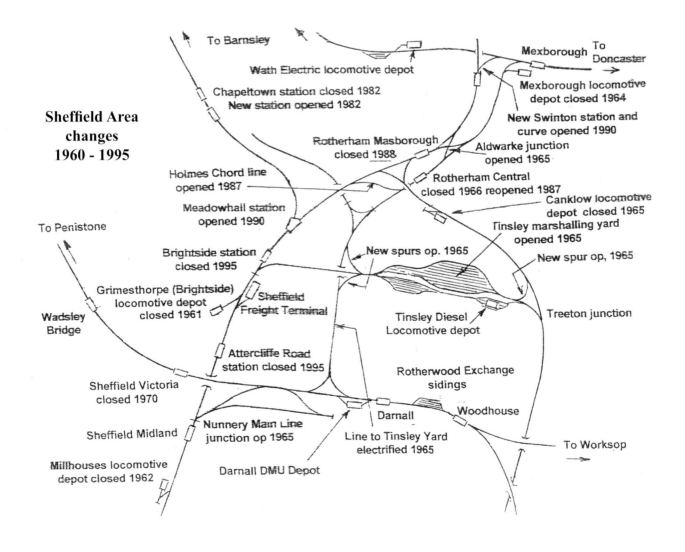

Sheffield Area changes 1960 - 1995

To Barnsley
Wath Electric locomotive depot
Chapeltown station closed 1982
New station opened 1982
Mexborough   To Doncaster
Mexborough locomotive depot closed 1964
New Swinton station and curve opened 1990
Rotherham Masborough closed 1988
Aldwarke junction opened 1965
Holmes Chord line opened 1987
Rotherham Central closed 1966 reopened 1987
Canklow locomotive depot closed 1965
Meadowhall station opened 1990
Tinsley marshalling yard opened 1965
To Penistone
Brightside station closed 1995
New spurs op. 1965
New spur op, 1965
Grimesthorpe (Brightside) locomotive depot closed 1961
Sheffield Freight Terminal
Treeton junction
Wadsley Bridge
Tinsley Diesel Locomotive depot
Attercliffe Road station closed 1995
Rotherwood Exchange sidings
Sheffield Victoria closed 1970
Darnall
Woodhouse
Sheffield Midland
Nunnery Main Line junction op 1965
Line to Tinsley Yard electrified 1965
To Worksop
Millhouses locomotive depot closed 1962
Darnall DMU Depot

10. Passenger services 1971 - 1982

By 1971 local services had been heavily rationalised with only 34 daily trains being run. The electric service had gone to be replaced by Huddersfield to Sheffield DMU trains which reversed at Nunnery to reach Sheffield Midland station. However the future of this service and that of the Clayton West branch trains was still uncertain. Long distance travel depended on connections at Huddersfield, Wakefield or Sheffield.

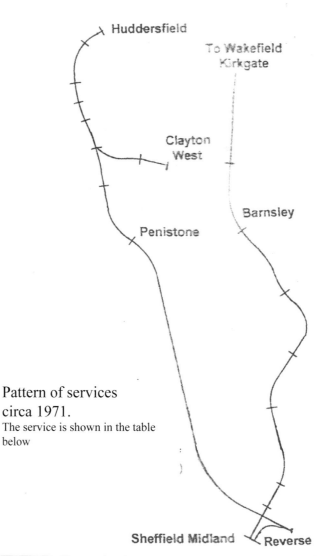

Pattern of services circa 1971.
The service is shown in the table below

Service operated	Railway company	Number of daily trains (one way)
Huddersfield - Penistone - Sheffield (local)	British Rail (Eastern)	11
Huddersfield - Clayton West.		5
Leeds - Normanton - Wakefield Kirkgate - Barnsley - Sheffield.		18
Total number of trains		34

A train for Sheffield formed by a class 101 DMU leaves Honley station in 1978 before the singling of this stretch of line. The Class 101 unit has an incorrect destination blind. Note the surviving ex LYR way out sign.

11. Second Penistone line closure case.

By 1976 the basis for calculating financial support for loss making local rail services had changed with the Cooper formula now being applied. This meant that the only passenger service using a line now had to bear the full track and infrastructure costs. As a result the subsidy required for the Sheffield to Penistone trains rose from £44,000 in 1970 to £610,000 in 1975. Not surprisingly SYPTE considered this cost to be out of all proportion to usage.

Therefore in 1976 in response to South Yorkshire County Council's difficulty in supporting it's share of the Sheffield to Penistone section of the Sheffield - Huddersfield passenger service British Railways carried out a study of alternatives and these were as follows:

Option 1 - The existing service on the present route.

Option 2 - An hourly service, 15 trains in each direction, each weekday, between Sheffield and Huddersfield, capable of operation on a single line, with additional stations at Wadsey Bridge, Outibridge and Deepcar.

Option 3 - An hourly service, 15 trains in each direction, each weekday, between Sheffield and Penistone only, capable of operation on a single line, with additional stations at Wadsey Bridge, Outibridge and Deepcar.

Option 4 - Existing level of service, operated between Sheffield and Huddersfield but routed via Barnsley and Penistone and calling only at Barnsley and Penistone in South Yorkshire.

	Option 1 £000's	Option 2 £000's	Option 3 £000's	Option 4 £000's
Train service & terminal expenses	115	160	155	148
Track, signal & admin expenses	546	315	320	230
Total expenses	661	475	475	378
Less earnings	33	90	65	60
Net deficit	628	385	410	318

The Huddersfield to Sheffield service was only months away from being closed and a last minute campaign was launched to save the line. In January 1983 British Railways issued the 'Time is running out' leaflet. Once the eleventh hour decision was made to retain the trains it was heavily promoted from both ends of the line to ensure it's success. Some of these leaflets are shown.

The PTE's considered their options for supporting local rail services. In 1977 South Yorkshire agreed to give Section 20 support to three local services as follows:

Route	Revenue	Costs	Net Deficit
Sheffield - Barnsley - Darton (- Leeds)	£145,000	£568,000	£423,000
Sheffield - Rotherham - Doncaster - Thorne	£422,000	£850,000	£428,000
Sheffield - Kiverton Park (- Lincoln)	£81,000	£327,000	£246,000
Totals	**£648,000**	**£1,745,000**	**£1,097,000**

West Yorkshire engaged Consultants to consider local services and the preliminary Wytconsult Study published in 1977 recommended that most local trains be retained and improved with 20 new stations except for Huddersfield to Clayton West and Penistone which it recommended for closure.

The Penistone line was now under threat and local group's and campaigners prepared for the closure battle to come which appeared from BR towards the end of 1980 and proposed closure of Clayton West Junction to Clayton West and Denby Dale to Sheffield Woodburn Junction. Stations would be closed at Skelmanthorpe, Clayton West and Penistone but a train service from Huddersfield to Denby Dale would continue with WYPTE support.

During 1981 the Transport Users Consultative Committee considered the closure proposal and received 547 written objections and then held a public inquiry. It's conclusions were that passengers using the Clayton West trains would suffer inconvenience but those travelling between Denby Dale and Sheffield would experience severe hardship and the proposed replacement bus services were not considered adequate.

The Minister of Transport's decision came on 21st. September 1982 giving consent to closure to Clayton West and also Denby Dale to Sheffield but the later was deferred to May 1983 to give SYPTE opportunity to agree Section 20 support.

West Yorkshire indicated that if South Yorkshire did not support the Penistone trains then support for the trains from Huddersfield would also be withdrawn. This would then be the end and the railway service from Huddersfield to Sheffield would disappear.

At the last minute South Yorkshire County Council on 2nd. March 1983 agreed a £400,000 grant to support Penistone line service via Barnsley for a 12 month experimental period. BR quickly upgraded the freight Penistone to Barnsley section of track to a line speed of 50 mph with improved signalling.

As this was only for a year and because West Yorkshire had indicated it's support depended on continuing support from South Yorkshire BR issued preliminary closure notices for the Huddersfield to Denby Dale part of the new service.

Despite this a joint marketing group of BR, WYPTE and SYPTE was formed to promote the new service. Much extra traffic was generated between Penistone and Barnsley. However WYPTE was now seeking a reduction of it's support payments arguing that the service acted as an inter city feeder and this again put the service at risk. It was not until late 1986 before this dispute was sorted out and the future of the service became secure. (Note TUCC closure enquiries were in October / November 1985)

Last day of operation of the Clayton West branch in 1983. The campaign to save the trains failed to save the branch British Railways expressed surprise at the closure inquiry how many people travelled from the growing town of Skelmanthorpe into Huddersfield but a decent rail service was not provided. Here the mid-day train formed by a Class 110 unit is shown which has been strengthened to 5 coaches to cater for enthusiasts making a last trip on the line.

Penistone line Branches

A train at the Meltham branch terminus in pre grouping days. An intensive service was operated until closure of the line to passengers in 1949. Freight traffic, which consisted largely of tractors from David Brown's works, continued until 1965.

Ivatt 2-6-2 tank number 41256 at Holmfirth station with a four car set of pregrouping rolling stock forms the local branch train for Huddersfield in 1952. The service was withdrawn in 1959.

Parcels are loaded onto the mid day train for Huddersfield at the terminal station at Clayton West in 1976. The train is formed by a two car Metropolitan Class 101 DMU. The branch closed to passengers in 1983 and to freight shortly after.

Summary Wine Scenery.

A Clayton West train in woodlands near Brockholes in 1978.

Honley station 2010.

A three car Class 144 unit forms a Sheffield to Huddersfield train between Denby Dale and Penistone on the curved single track section through superb pennine scenery in 2010.   Emley Moor transmitter mast can be seen in the top left hand corner.

A Class 144 crosses Oxspring viaduct in 2004.

A Huddersfield to Sheffield train calla at Shepley station in 1988.

Ex - LNER Express trains.

The up South Yorkshireman unusually headed by a Class B1 4-6-0 No. 61061 crosses Penistone viaduct in 1954. The train was booked to be worked to Sheffield by a Bradford (Low Moor) LMS 5MT 4-6-0 but in this instance something appears to gave gone awry since the train engine is not only a B1 but one from far-off Darlington! Photo: Initial Photographics.

Two types of Electric locomotives were built for the Woodhead electrification. EM1 (later Class 76) for freight and EM2 (later Class 77) for express passenger. Here EM2 No. 27001 at Penistone in 1954 with a Manchester to Marylebone express.   In spite of the differences, both classes were regarded as one for goods workings.   Photo: Ken Nunn collection.

In British Railway days a number of A3 Pacifics worked the Great Central expresses from Sheffield and Manchester.   Here No. 60102 'Sir Fredrick Banbury' arrives at London Marylebone with the South Yorkshireman in 1953, having taken over the train at Leicester.. Photo: AGF / Initial Photographics.

Ex - LMS Express trains.

Ex LMS Jubilee class 4-6-0 No. 45602 'British Honduras' pauses at Sheffield Midland station in 1956 with a Midland Main Line express. The class was the mainstay of Midland express trains until 1957 when, for five years, they were augmented by a number of 7P Britannia Pacifics and Royal Scot 4-6-0's. Picture D.K. Jones.

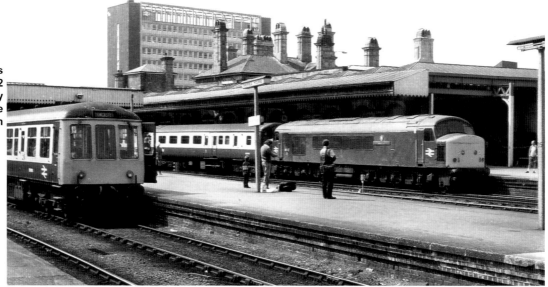

The Midland express services were dieselised in the 1962 with trains being worked by Sulzer 2500hp Type 4's. Here 45137 pauses at Sheffield with a Midland express in 1984.

An Inter-city High Speed Train (HST) forms a service for London St. Pancras at Sheffield in 1986. These units superseded the Sulzer Type 4 locomotives from 1979 on Midland line and cross country expresses.

12. 1980's rationalisation

During this period British Railways were under great pressure to reduce costs and considered major route rationalisation and closures to remove surplus capacity. At an internal consultation meeting on 3rd. August 1983 no less than 237 lines were listed nationally involving the possible closure and removal of 1,917 miles of track.

These show the serious consideration being given to reducing costs. Surprise proposals were to single the Calder Valley main line between Milner Royd junction and Heaton Lodge junction and the trans-pennine main line from Thornhill LNW junction to Dewsbury station. Neither was carried out but many were although the Penistone line retained double track between Shepley and Stocksmoor.

The following were relevant to the routes we are considering.

'A' Elimination of non-essential multiple tracks.

Between	Proposal	Track reductions
Milner Royd junction - Heaton Lodge	single	7 miles
Milner Royd junction - Bowling junction	single	10 miles
Dearne Valley N junction - Royston junction	dequadrify	11 miles
Clayton West junction - Springwood junction	single	6 miles
Thornhill LNW junction - Dewsbury	single	2 miles
Heaton Lodge junction - Thornhill LNW junction	dequadrify	5 miles
Quarry junction - Stairfoot junctionn	single	1 miles
Elsecar junction - Wath Central junction	single	4 miles
Huddersfield junction - Dodworth	single	4 miles
Deepcar - Woodburn junction	single	9 miles
Sheffield Victoria Woodhouse junction	dequadrify	10 miles

'B' Routes identified for Closure and now out of use.

Between	Route miles	Track miles
Low Moor - Thornhill	7	8.6
Clayton West Branch	3.3	3.4

'C' Routes identified for Closure and currently in use.

Between	Route	Track
Aldham junction - Dovecliffe	1.45	3
Stairfoot junction - Cudworth	1.05	2.2
Stairfoot junction - Elsecar	3.5	7.2
Huddersfield junction - Deepcar	5	10
Wath Rd junction - Dearne Valley junction	5	10

Diversion via Barnsley.

The Huddersfield to Sheffield trains were rerouted via Barnsley in 1983 after a long campaign to save them. The suggested diversion came from local transport pressure group Transport 2000 of which I was the Secretary at the time. It was clear that without this the service would have certainly closed. British Railways reacted in a positive manner to this suggestion and although tight lipped ran a special trial train along the proposed new route. We learnt from the train driver, as ASLEF was affiliated to Transport 2000, about the special run and that British Railways were happy with the trial and considered it a success.

It was not known at this time that a few years later Meadowhall would open to give a massive boost to the service which would not have been possible had the trains stayed on the original route.

It is a pity however that we did not persuade Metro and British Railways to retain the Clayton West branch service   This would have provided a more frequent service for all stations between Huddersfield and Shepley plus serving the sizable settlement of Skelmanthorpe as well as ensuring retention of more track capacity.

13. South Yorkshire Developments

Although South Yorkshire took a cautious approach in taking responsibility for local train services once these had been put on a sound footing it joined with West Yorkshire PTE in developing services and thus reversing the long period of decline with the major developments as follows:.

1982 - relocation of Chapeltown station.
1984 - Silkstone Common station opened
1987 - opening of a new Rotherham Central station and a new Holmes chord line.
1988 - Introduction of new Leeds - Sheffield local service via Moorthorpe by West Yorkshire and South Yorkshire PTE's including the opening of Thurnscoe and Goldthorpe stations.
1989 - opening of Dodworth station in South Yorkshire and Berry Brow station in West Yorkshire.
1990 - opening of Swinton station and a new curve plus the opening of Meadowhall station.

(Note; In West Yorkshire the line was singled from Stocksmoor to Springwood junction in 1989 to enable a relocated Berry Brow station to be opened. This was a significant change to the line to also reduce Section 20 costs.)

14. Tram - Train on the Penistone line.

The Penistone line was a former main line which carried 'The South Yorkshireman' express but was proposed for closure by Beeching although later reprieved. However it continued to operate in a run down condition carrying a Huddersfield - Penistone - Barnsley - Sheffield local service using a severely rationalised mostly single track route between Huddersfield and Barnsley. Despite this the service has prospered carrying 1.2 million annual passengers in 2007 compared with 500,000 in 1993.

In a boost for the area the Government announced in 2008 that it would sponsor a Tram - Train trial over the Penistone line to test possible applications in the UK of this technology which has been very successful in Germany. This involves trams running on existing heavy railways until reaching the town centre where they would branch off to commence street running.

The first phase was for a tram service using existing stations between Huddersfield and Sheffield for a two year trial period starting in 2010. This would have involved the lowering of platforms or new ones at 17 stations. On completion of this the next phase was to build a connection from the existing railway to link up with the Sheffield Supertram system so that the trams could run into Sheffield city centre.

It soon became clear that this link up was not feasible so the second phase was changed to run between Rotherham and Sheffield. As the project progressed further major problems began to emerge with difficulties procuring diesel - electric tram trains which were dubbed 'unaffordable'. Plans prepared for the stations showed that 12 stations would need lower platform extensions, 4 stations would need new platforms and at Huddersfield, Sheffield and Penistone the existing platforms would need to be lowered.

It was therefore not surprising when in 2009 the Government announced that the full trial would be switched to a Rotherham to Sheffield electrified tram - train scheme with the Penistone line project put 'on hold'/

A Sheffield to Huddersfield train calls at the new single platform station at Berry Brow in 1989. The train is formed by one of the 20 Class 141 lightweight unit introduced into West Yorkshire in 1984. These and the later Class 142 units were built from bus bodies and were thus very much like a tram vehicle.

A train for Sheffield stands in Platform 2 at Huddersfield station in 2009. This bay platform was specially created in 1990 for the Sheffield service to improve reliability by keeping the service separate from trans-pennine express services. The former long discarded bay platform can be seen on the left.

A train from Sheffield leaves Springwood junction and enters Huddersfield station tunnel in 1983. It can be seen that the train will cross the Manchester line to gain access to the station and trains had often to wait for this to be clear. Alterations in 1990 created a new bay platform 2 with trains using separate tracks enabling the Sheffield service to work independently of other trains. However a connection with the other tracks in the station was provided to enable a train per day to run through to Leeds.

A Sheffield bound DMU crosses the extensive Lockwood viaduct in 1978. This is one of the largest viaducts in England with 34 arches towering some 136 feet above the River Holme. The trackbed has since been reduced to single track.

15. The Route today.

Most trains leave the dedicated platform 2 bay platform at Huddersfield station to immediately enter the Huddersfield South tunnel before diverging as a single track from the main Manchester line at Springwood junction. Immediately following is the 15 arch stone and lattice girder Paddock viaduct which crosses both the Huddersfield & Ashton Canal and the River Colne. Next is Lockwood tunnel after which we come immediately into Lockwood station. This uses a single platform although the other

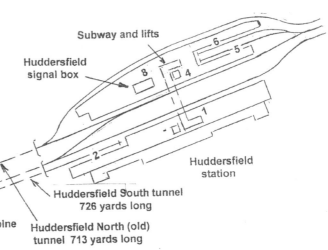

Subway and lifts

Huddersfield signal box

Huddersfield station

Huddersfield South tunnel 726 yards long

Huddersfield North (old) tunnel 713 yards long

to Manchester

River Colne

Lockwood station

Paddock viaduct

Former branch to Meltham

Lockwood tunnel 205 yards long

River Holme

Lockwood viaduct

Robin Hood tunnel 228 yards long

Berry Brow station

Honley Tunnel 42 yards long

Honley station

Brockholes station

Thurstonland tunnel 1631 yards long

Former branch to Holmfirth

Stocksmoor station

Shepley station

Cumberworth tunnel 906 yards long

Former branch to Clayton West (now Kirklees Light Railway)

Denby Dale station

Denby Dale viaduct

Wellhouse tunnel 415 yards long

platform remains but now without track. Currently the Penistone line only has a hourly service and should this be improved in the future then this disused platform and a passing loop would need to be brought back into use.

Lockwood viaduct which carries the single track railway 136 feet above the River Holme is next. After passing through a rock cutting we reach the reopened and relocated Berry Brow station with the single platform having been built on the former up track bed which will make any future restoration to double track more difficult. Two short tunnels follow before we enter a heavily rationalised Honley station. This is the worst station on the route with a single platform, poor waiting facilities and terrible access.

Thurstonland tunnel, which is the longest on the line, is traversed next after which we come to the two mile double track section which includes stations at Stocksmoor and Shepley with it's staggered platforms. This is the section on which timetabled trains pass each other and any significant delay to one train will be passed on to the other.

Upon rejoining the single track the control of trains now passes from Huddersfield to Barnsley signal box. After Cumberworth tunnel our train enters Denby Dale station. At one time this station had quite lavish facilities but was singled in 1969 with railway land sold off leaving a cramped single platform station. Immediately leaving the station we cross the impressive Denby Dale viaduct then Wellhouse tunnel on the final 4 miles to Penistone.

Just before Penistone station is Penistone viaduct which is the first of three crossings of the River Don. The station itself has two platforms and a passing loop which is now much reduced from the previous six platform extensive station and sidings.

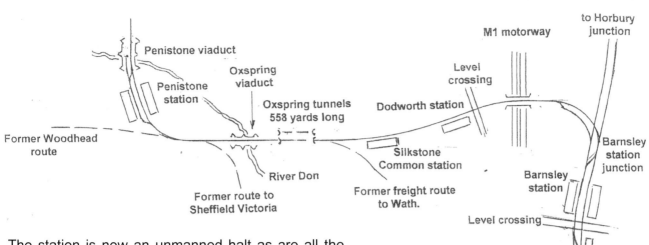

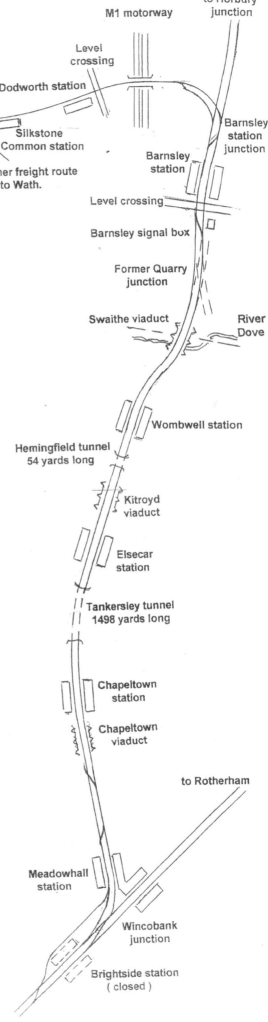

The station is now an unmanned halt as are all the other intermediate stations except Barnsley and Meadowhall. On leaving Penistone the single line runs for a short stretch on the former Great Central main line then over Oxspring viaduct before entering one of the twin bores of Oxspring tunnel, the other being disused.

Next is the single platform Silkstone Common station reopened in 1984 followed by Dodworth station which similarly reopened 5 years later. After the station is the level crossing now controlled by Barnsley signal box and on the left is an industrial estate which stands on the site of Dodworth colliery. The M1 motorway is crossed by a single track girder bridge. Had the freight route not remained open when the motorway was built the route would have been severed and reinstatement of the passenger service would have been prohibitive.

As we approach Barnsley the line changes to double track as we descend a curved 1 in 50 gradient to Barnsley Station junction and into the station. This gradient can cause the wheels of trains ascending the bank to slip in greasy conditions. Today Barnsley station is at the centre of a state of the art transport interchange where passengers can make seamless transfer between buses and trains.

After Barnsley station is a level crossing and we then pass Barnsley signalbox which controls the signalling on much of the route. Just outside Barnsley we pass the site of the former Quarry junction where in 1960 a connection was made to enable trains to join the ex-Midland route to Sheffield Midland. The track has all been realigned and there is now no evidence of the variation in levels or extensive junction or multiple tracks that once existed here.

We then pass over Swaithe viaduct which carries the line over the former Worsborough freight line which is now a footpath. Next is Wombwell station followed by Hemingfield tunnel and Kitroyd viaduct before entering Elsecar station. Tankerrsley tunnel follows before reaching the new Chapeltown

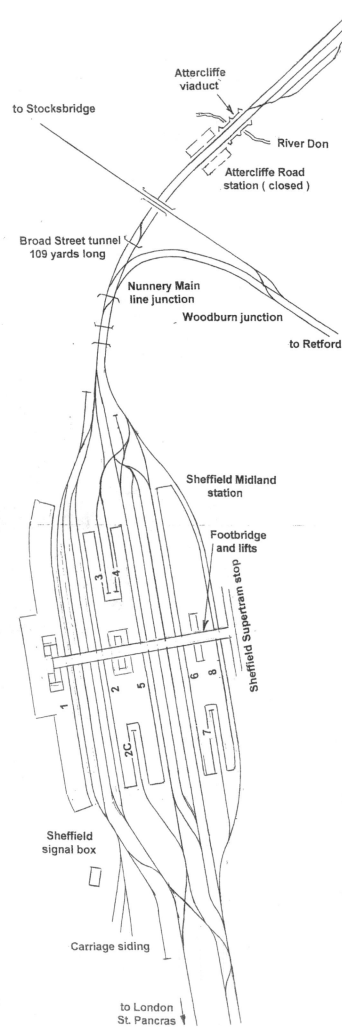

to Stocksbridge

Attercliffe viaduct

River Don

Attercliffe Road station (closed)

Broad Street tunnel 109 yards long

Nunnery Main line junction

Woodburn junction

to Retford

Sheffield Midland station

Footbridge and lifts

Sheffield Supertram stop

3 4

6 8

2 5

1

7

2C

Sheffield signal box

Carriage siding

to London St. Pancras

station which was re-sited in 1982 to a more accessible location some 200 yards south of the original station. Immediately after the station is Chapeltown viaduct which elevates the railway across the town centre.

Just before reaching Meadowhall the control of trains passes from Barnsley to Sheffield signal box. In fact the route is operated very efficiently with modern colour light signals operated from just three signal boxes. The line then continues to join the former Midland Railway north - south main line at the four platform Meadowhall station opened in 1990. This was built to serve the adjacent Meadowhall shopping centre but it also serves as an interchange point and has become one of the most important stations in South Yorkshire.

We next pass Brightside station which is closed but still mainly intact . This section of the route has been greatly reduced from four to two tracks but a few sidings and passing loops still remain until we approach Attercliffe viaduct where we again cross the River Don and then immediately pass the closed Attercliffe Road station. Broad Street tunnel and Nunnery Main Line junction complete the journey into Sheffield. Even when greater capacity existed the two track section over Attercliffe viaduct then through Attercliffe Road station and the tunnel into Sheffield always provided a restriction to trains.

Sheffield station although modernised retains it's basic layout from Midland Railway days. However today it is part of the Sheffield Interchange with adjacent bus station and adjoining Supertram stop at the side of the station.

Santa Specials.
Leaflet of festive 'Santa Special' party and music trains ran in 2009 to promote the service.

16. Huddersfield station

Huddersfield is quite rare in that it has only ever had one central railway station although a Midland Railway station was planned but never materialised as a passenger station but emerged as a goods depot. Huddersfield station was opened by a local company before being taken over by the London & North Western Railway and provided with a magnificent station façade which faces on to St. Georges Square. It later became a joint station with the Lancashire & Yorkshire Railway who ran their trains into and through the station rather than building their own separate station.

Huddersfield is thus located on the main trans-pennine main line with excellent east - west rail links. Because of these Lancashire and Yorkshire rugby clubs chose the George Hotel in St. Georges Square next to Huddersfield station for the historic 1895 meeting at which northern clubs broke away from the Rugby Union to form the Northern Union later to become the Rugby Football League.

Huddersfield station 1987 A Class 144 unit forms a train for Sheffield at Platform 4. Prior to the opening of the new bay platform 2 trains departed from this platform but had to cross the path of Manchester bound trans-pennine trains leading to delays. 4 through tracks are still in use in this view.

A 2009 exterior view of the magnificent Huddersfield station with it's original frontage facing St. Georges Square and now fronted by a statue of Harold Wilson who was born in Huddersfield and was Prime Minister from 1964 to 1970 and 1974 to 1976. The station was jointly owned by the LNWR and LYR.

17. Penistone stations

The first station was provided by the Sheffield, Ashton under Lyne & Manchester Railway on the Manchester to Sheffield line opened in 1845 in the town centre. The S, A & M became the Manchester, Sheffield & Lincolnshire Railway in 1847 and then the Great Central in 1897. The Lancashire & Yorkshire route from Huddersfield reached Penistone in 1850 with a station at the junction with the M, S & L line.

From 1874 the first Penistone station was replaced by a new station 0.5 miles to the east at Huddersfield junction to form a new combined station with the LYR. After the collapse of two arches of Penistone viaduct in February 1916 a temporary Penistone (Barnsley Road) halt was opened where trains from Huddersfield terminated until 14th. August 1916.

Electric trains served the station from 1954 until 1970 when the Manchester platforms where closed but their overgrown remains can still be seen today. The canopies and overhead electric gantries have been removed but the station building remains in use today as offices. The former Woodhead line has been converted into a footpath which runs through the former station giving good access to the remaining part of the station.

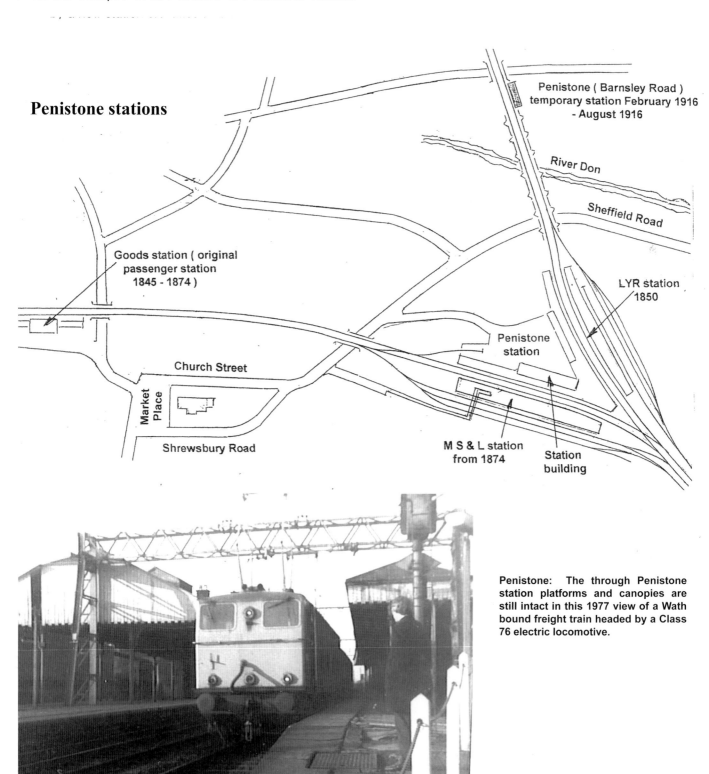

Penistone stations

Penistone (Barnsley Road) temporary station February 1916 - August 1916

River Don

Sheffield Road

Goods station (original passenger station 1845 - 1874)

LYR station 1850

Penistone station

Church Street

Market Place

Shrewsbury Road

M S & L station from 1874

Station building

Penistone: The through Penistone station platforms and canopies are still intact in this 1977 view of a Wath bound freight train headed by a Class 76 electric locomotive.

18. Barnsley stations

The first station to carry the name Barnsley was at Cudworth on the North Midland Railway's (later Midland Railway) Derby to Leeds main line opened in 1840. A local company, later taken over by the Lancashire and Yorkshire Railway, opened a line from Horbury Junction to a Barnsley Regent Street station (later Exchange) in 1850. Lines from Mexborough reached Barnsley in 1851 and from Penistone in 1859 both of which later became part of the Great Central Railway. Finally in 1870 the Midland Railway Cudworth to Barnsley branch line was completed while at the same time the main line station was renamed Cudworth with a connecting service to Barnsley provided.

The Railway Company acquired the old Barnsley Court House building and this was opened as the new Court House station in 1873 to replace a temporary station. Barnsley then had two town centre stations. Barnsley Exchange which had a single platform and accommodated Lancashire & Yorkshire trains from Wakefield Kirkgate and the main Court House station which had two through platforms and a Penistone facing bay. This was served by competing Midland and Great Central trains to Sheffield, a through Doncaster to Penistone service and a shuttle to connect with main line trains at Cudworth. Despite it's name the Hull & Barnsley Railway never reached Barnsley.

From the mid 1950's uneconomic services were beginning to be axed and the remaining trains dieselised. By 1960 most of the Court House station's trains had been withdrawn leaving only a solitary diesel operated Barnsley to Sheffield service. Similarly at Exchange station a Leeds via Wakefield Kirkgate and Normanton diesel service remained. British Railways proposed to link these up to form a new Sheffield to Leeds service.

Court House station was built on a viaduct and needed £200,000 spent on it in 1960. In view of the limited use of the station British Railways decided to close it and concentrate the planned through service on Exchange station. As there was no direct connection between the former Midland and GC lines a new connecting line was installed at Quarry junction. This involved a quarter mile of new track with substantial earthworks to raise the level of track by up to 14 feet in places. As part of the same scheme an additional through platform was built at Barnsley Exchange.

Today Exchange station is simply called Barnsley and is part of a modern transport interchange. Little remains of the former elevated Court Hose station but the station building remains and is now a public house called appropriately 'The Court House' and a small section of the original viaduct can still be seen..

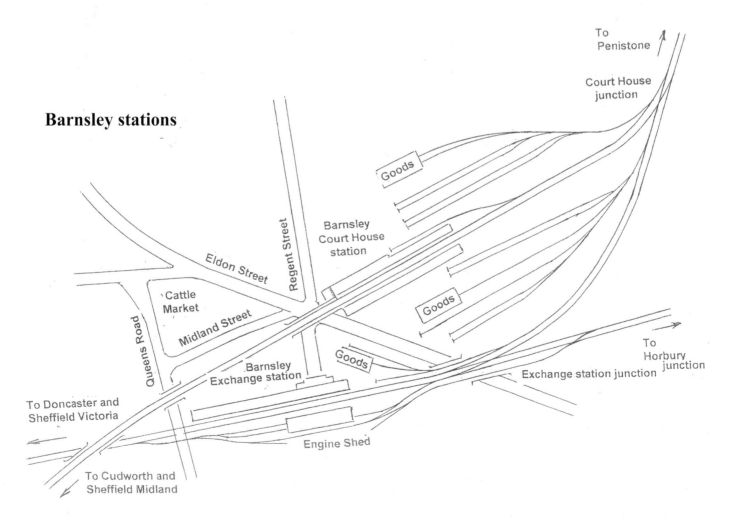

Barnsley stations

Barnsley stations.

The first Barnsley station was on the main line at Cudworth until 1870 when the branch to Barnsley was opened and the main line station was renamed Cudworth. Here a Jubilee class locomotive calls at the station with a northbound express in 1953. Passengers continued to change here for Barnsley until closure in 1958. Photo: Stations UK.

Barnsley Court House station opened in 1873 and became the town's main station until 1960. The station had decent passenger facilities with an overall roof and footbridge. Here an Ivatt class 2-6-2 tank locomotive forms the two coach push and pull shuttle service for Cudworth in 1953 where it would connect with main line trains. Photo: Stations UK/

A view of Barnsley Court House station from the north east in 1958 The bay platform can be seen on the right. A new Diesel Multiple unit has just arrived from Sheffield stand in the following year would become the only service using the station after withdrawal of the remaining steam services from Penistone, Doncaster and Cudworth. Photo: Stations UK.

A view of Barnsley Exchange station in 1955. There were two running lines at this location but the station only had a single platform used by trains to Wakefield Kirkgate. The walls of the ex GC two-lane engine shed which had an allocation of around forty engines can be seen on the left. The shed was demolished in 1960 nd the space used to erect a second platform. Photo: Stations UK.

A Sheffield to Leeds DMU at Barnsley Exchange station in 1982. In this view the original station building and platform are still standing on the left hand side. The extra platform and waiting shelter built in 1960 on the site of the old engine shed can be seen on the right. This was to accommodate services displaced when Court House station was closed.

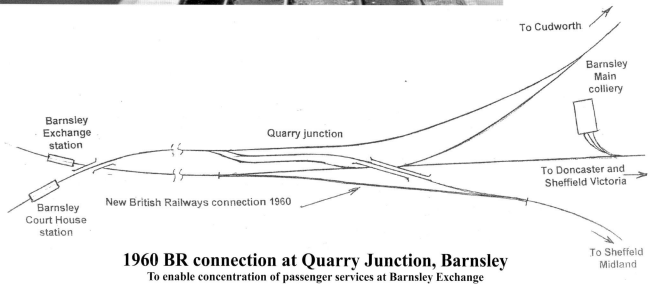

1960 BR connection at Quarry Junction, Barnsley
To enable concentration of passenger services at Barnsley Exchange

Former Quarry junction 2010.

A Class 144 unit forms a Huddersfield to Sheffield local service on the new connecting line built by British Railways in 1960. The skewing of the tracks to accommodate the different levels is clearly visible.

Barnsley Interchange 2010.

A Leeds - Nottingham train formed by a Class 158 unit leaves Barnsley Interchange station in 2010. The adjacent bus station built on the old Court House Railway viaduct is on the left and Barnsley signal box on the right.

19. Sheffield stations

The first Sheffield station opened in 1838 at Wicker as the terminus of the first railway from Rotherham. Bridgehouses station opened next in 1845 as the terminal station of the Sheffield , Ashton under Lyne and Manchester Railway. Both these stations were soon replaced and became goods depots, Sheffield Victoria for Bridgehouses in 1851 and Sheffield Midland took over services from Wicker station in 1870 when the new loop line from Chesterfield to Rotherham was opened.

For many years timetables showed the Midland station simply as Sheffield but to distinguish it from Victoria, it was often locally referred to as Midland station although occasionally one would hear it described as Pond Street station - something of a misnomer since the station was in Sheaf Street. After an abortive proposal to name in 'Sheffield City',

the respective names of Midland and Victoria were given official sanction in 1951. Midland station was eventually to become the only city centre station when all passenger traffic became concentrated at the station. A new curve was opened at Nunnery and from October 4th. 1965 services from Lincoln were diverted to Midland station rather than Sheffield Victoria. The Manchester electrics continued to use Victoria until 1970 when the station was closed and a diesel service from Huddersfield and Penistone replaced the electrics and ran into Midland station after reversal at Woodburn junction..

After the closure of Victoria station Midland station reverted to the simple title of Sheffield and has more recently been modernised to become part of the Sheffield Interchange complex with a connecting walkway to the city bus station and an adjacent Supertram station stop connection via the footbridge.

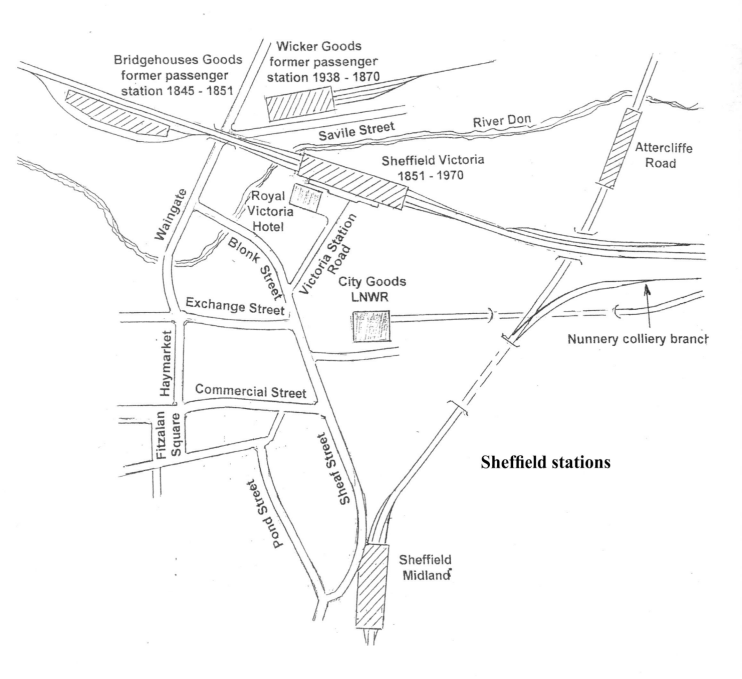

Sheffield stations

Sheffield Midland Diesel.

An overall view of Sheffield Midland station in 1977. A Class 40 diesel locomotive propels a parcel train out of the station bound for the Rotherham direction. The dominating office block has now been abolished, the station revamped and the road and parked cars in the foreground have now been replaced by the route of the Sheffield supertram.

A class 45 diesel locomotive at Sheffield Midland station in 1977 after arrival with a train from London St. Pancras. The locomotives were the mainstay of this service from the end of steam until the arrival of the HST's.

Sheffield Midland steam.

Sheffield Midland station 1955. Arrival of 12.30 from Barnsley Court House headed by 2-4-2 tank no. 50646. The overall roof, since removed, can be seen in this picture. Photo: Initial Photographics.

Class 5 4-6-0 no. 44665 and 2-6-2 tank no. 40181 at Sheffield Midland in 1953. The overall roof and footbridge are in view. Photo: BWLB / Initial Photographics.

British Railways Standard Class 4 4-6-0 locomotive no. 75064 arrives at Sheffield Midland station in 1961. Photo: D.K. Jones

Sheffield Victoria Station

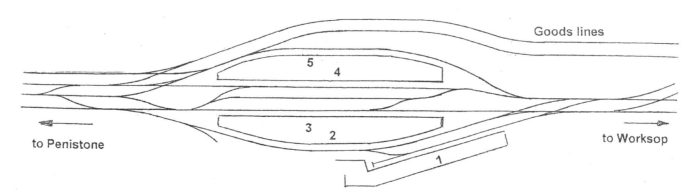

Class B17 4-6-0 locomotive number 61660 'Hull City' heads the Harwich boat train at Sheffield Victoria in 1951. This was one of the crack express trains through Sheffield running from Manchester to East Anglia and was booked to a March B17 4-6-0 locomotive. Passengers on the train could not complain about a lack of motive power variety with a Black 5 from Liverpool to Manchester Central, an LMS 2-6-4T to Guide Bridge, an EM2 electric to Sheffield, a B17 4-6-0 to March and a B1 4-6-0 for the remainder of the journey! Photo. Initial Photographs / BWLB

Ex LNER Class B1 number 61158 at Sheffield Victoria with a RCTS (Railway Correspondence and Travel Society) special in 1964. Picture: D.K. Jones.

20. Present day train services

Services have been greatly improved with Express trains introduced between Leeds, Barnsley and Sheffield in 2004. Sunday services were reintroduced on the Penistone line in May 1988 with further improved in 2008. There was also a significant improvement in the weekday service frequency at this time. However the greatest effect came with the opening of Meadowhall station in 1990. This has since developed into one of the most important stations in South Yorkshire.   Not only does it serve the shopping centre but has also become an interchange station between the Barnsley line and Rotherham lines as well as local bus services.   No less than 149 trains per day in each direction serve Meadowhall.   Train connections possible are shown in the hourly pattern of services.

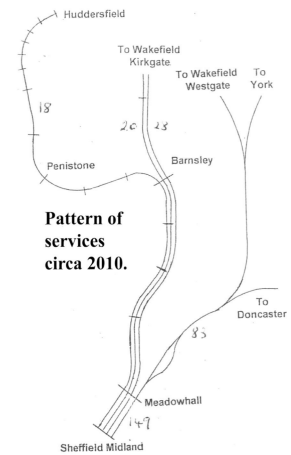

Pattern of services circa 2010.

Service operated	Railway company	Number of daily trains (one way)
Huddersfield - Penistone - Barnsley - Sheffield (local)	Northern Rail	18
Leeds - Normanton - Castleford - Wakefield Kirkgate - Barnsley - Sheffield.		20
Leeds - Wakefield - Barnsley - Sheffield (express)		28
Doncaster / York / Leeds / Rotherham - Meadowhall - Sheffield		83
Total number of trains		**149**

Hourly pattern of services.

	Ex	Ex	L	Ex	L	L	L	L	Ex
Doncaster	09.42	09.48			09.58			10.24	
Rotherham					10.27		10.44	10.50	
Sheffield			10.06	10.18		10.36			10.51
Meadowhall	10.01	10.06	10.12	10.24	10.37	10.42	10.50	10.55	10.57
Barnsley			10.32	10.40		11.01			11.11
Penistone						11.18			
Huddersfield						11.49			
Leeds			11.25	11.18					11.48

	L	L	Ex	L	L	Ex	Ex	L	Ex
Leeds			09.37		09.32		10.05		
Huddersfield	09.13								
Penistone	09.44								
Barnsley	10.01		10.14		10.24		10.40		
Meadowhall	10.19	10.21	10.27	10.3	10.46	10.47	10.52	11.03	11.17
Sheffield	10.30		10.37		10.56		11.02		
Rotherham		10.27		10.37				11.10	
Doncaster			11.04		11.11			11.36	11.40

Ex Express train,   **L** - local stopping train

Railway Privatisation - 1

The railways were privatised in 1994 and the Midland Main Line company ran the St. Pancras services until 2007 when East Midlands Trains took over. Here a Midland Main Line HST pauses at Sheffield Midland station in 2000.

Virgin Trains ran cross country express trains again until 2007 when Arriva Cross Country took over. Here a Virgin HST leaves Sheffield with a Bristol to Newcastle cross country express.

Both East Midland Trains and Virgin ordered new trains for both routes. Here Class 220 / 221 units form a northbound cross country express in 2009.

Midland Main Line introduced a St. Pancras to Barnsley service which ran from 2000 until 2007. Here a Class 170 units forms a mid day London to Barnsley service as it calls at Meadowhall station in 2000.

East Midland Trains took over the operation of the Midland main line from MML in 2007. Here a Class 223 unit forms a train for London St. Pancras at Sheffield station in 2010. The service was increased to two trains per hour between Sheffield and London St. Pancras from 2009.

Local services after BR in 1996 were run by Merseyside bus company MTL then
Arriva Trains Northern (Northern Spirit) until 2005 when the present Northern Rail company started to run the trains. Here a class 144 unit forms a Northern Sheffield to Huddersfield service near Penistone in 2010.

Railway Infrastructure.

Typical pre grouping scene of junctions and signals. This is Wincobank Station Junction with the line to Chapeltown and Barnsley diverging to the left from the Midland main line to Leeds and Carlisle. Beyond the station were the huge Wincobank up and down yards which dealt with loaded coal traffic and empty mineral wagons respectively. Picture Lens of Sutton.

An overhead view of the viaduct at the south side of Barnsley Court House station in 1958. 58066 is running round it's train for Sheffield Midland. The bus station can be seen on the left Following the ending of the Barnsley trams in the 1930's motor bus services expanded to served the town. The site of the viaduct and old bus station was used to form the present Interchange. Picture: Transport Treasury.

Level crossing: A Class 142 unit bound for Huddersfield passes over the level crossing at Dodworth in 1989. The signal box and crossing cabin is on the right. Conbtrol of the crossing has since been transferred to Barnsley signal box.

21. Routes through the coalfields

The whole area served by this railway stands on numerous coal seams and in the nineteenth century this supported hundreds of small collieries stretching all the way from Huddersfield to Sheffield. Gradually most of these became uneconomic as the demand for coal was met from a smaller number of larger pits as the coalfield receded and concentrated mainly on the Barnsley seams. With nationalisation in 1948 the National Coal Board was formed who invested in mechanisation to improve output from the remaining 'super pits'. However the mining industry was severely damaged by the 1984 - 1985 miners strike and by 1992 all had closed to be subsequently raised to the ground with the spoil heaps levelled and landscaped.

The railway was closely related to the coal industry with most local lines built to transport coal. The industry provided large revenues for the railway companies and without doubt this traffic kept open passengers services for many years. It is unlikely that the Huddersfield to Sheffield passenger service would have survived had not the coal traffic from Emley Moor and Dodworth collieries contributed to keeping open lines at Penistone and Barnsley into the 1980's.

However the other side of the coin was that mining caused subsidence for the railways particularly effecting the main lines. Of particular concern was the Midland main line which was closed to passenger trains in 1968 when expresses were diverted via Moorthorpe. However following agreement between BR and the NCB the Cudworth route was reinstated in 1972 but in 1984 this again reverted back to the Moorthorpe route which became the Leeds to Sheffield main line.

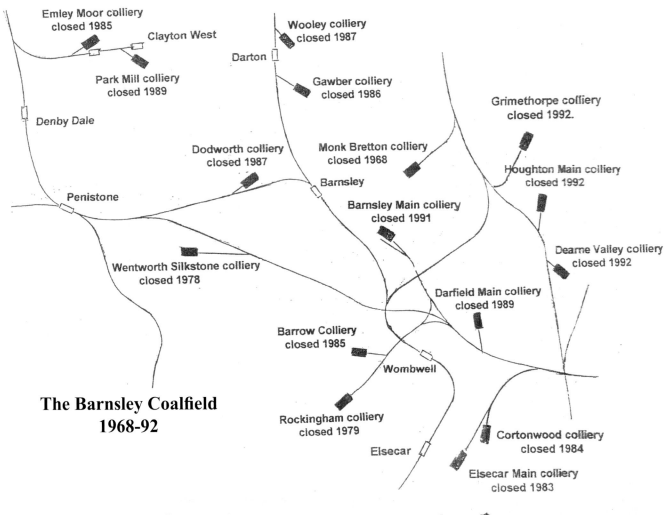

The Barnsley Coalfield 1968-92

Class 37 diesel locomotive 37040 making up a train for Healey Mills at Park Mill colliery near Clayton West. In 1977. Picture: Gavin Morrison.

Local collieries.

A Sheffield to Huddersfield train passes Dodworth Colliery in 1983. The importance of coal traffic in the region cannot be understated and support from the coal traffic helped to sustain this railway route long enough for it to be retained for the diverted service. The colliery finally closed in 1987 and the site has now been cleared.

A Clayton West branch train formed by a Class 101 DMU calls at the single platform Skelmanthorpe station in 1978. The 16-ton all-steel mineral wagons which became standard for coal traffic from the mid-sixties, can be seen in the adjacent Emley Moor Colliery sidings.

Movement of coal

The main traffic over Woodhead is coal for Fiddler's Ferry power station in Cheshire but the coal is no longer entirely local and is moving away from the Woodhead route. Coal concentration plans by the National Coal Board mean that future coal flows will be better moved by the Diggle route. The future trend will be for less coal crossing the Pennines.

BR proposals (1979) for the futiure movement of coal using the Diggle route.

COAL CONCENTRATION

HEALEY MILLS

WOOLLEY

GRIMETHORPE

BARNSLEY

HOUGHTON

WATH

22. Manchester - Sheffield / Wath electrification.

The Great Central main line across the pennines carried heavy passenger and freight traffic particularly coal from the South Yorkshire pits and steel from Sheffield. It was therefore an ideal candidate for electrification and this was first considered in 1926. However it was 10 years later before work started but this was halted by the second world war.

Work resumed after the end of the war but a major obstacle was the condition of the two Woodhead tunnels which consisted of two single bores constructed in 1845 and 1852. There was therefore little alternative but to construct a new one alongside and the new double track tunnel, which became the third longest in Britain, was opened in 1954.

Although the line escaped the first Beeching axe a second report in 1967 proposed that passenger traffic between Manchester and Sheffield should be concentrated on the Hope Valley route with the Woodhead line used for freight. In 1965 there was an extension of the electrification from Sheffield to the new Tinsley marshalling yard.. There were 55 westbound

and 46 eastbound freight trains using the ex GC route in 1967 As a result the electric passenger service was withdrawn at the start of 1970 leaving only a DMU service between Penistone and Sheffield.

On 7th. October 1980 British Railways announced it's intention to close completely the Woodhead route between Penistone and Hadfield claiming that this would save £2.5 million per year. The Board pointed out that the electrification at 1,500 volts DC was an outdated system and freight movement was down to 25 daily trains each way and forecast to fall further which could be accommodated on the three remaining trans-pennine routes.

The closure was effective from 20th. July 1981 followed by the section from Penistone to Deepcar in 1983 when the Huddersfield DMU's were diverted to run via Barnsley. This left the only part of the original route remaining open being from Sheffield to Deepcar and this was de-electrified, singled and connected to the Stocksbridge railway as a siding for the traffic from the steel works.

Two class 76 EM1 electric locomotives head a merry go round train of Yorkshire coal for Fiddlers Ferry power station over the Woodhead line in 1978. The route was to close completely three years later when coal trains became diesel operated and were diverted over the ex-LNWR Standedge route.

Official opening of the new Woodhead tunnel by the Minister of Transport on 3rd, June 1954. The first train through the tunnel was EM1 locomotive number 26020 shown here. This locomotive had been exhibited at the Festival of Britain in 1951. Picture: Transport Treasury.

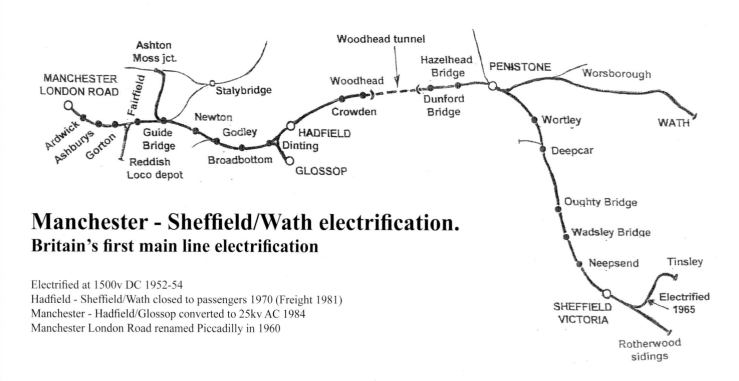

Manchester - Sheffield/Wath electrification.
Britain's first main line electrification

Electrified at 1500v DC 1952-54
Hadfield - Sheffield/Wath closed to passengers 1970 (Freight 1981)
Manchester - Hadfield/Glossop converted to 25kv AC 1984
Manchester London Road renamed Piccadilly in 1960

, , , , , and closure.

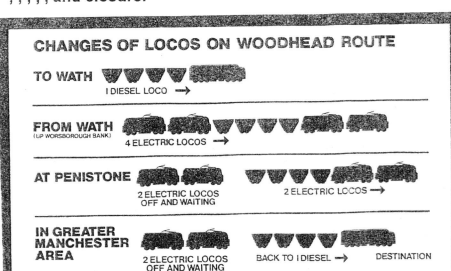

CHANGES OF LOCOS ON WOODHEAD ROUTE

TO WATH — I DIESEL LOCO →

FROM WATH (UP WORSBOROUGH BANK) — 4 ELECTRIC LOCOS →

AT PENISTONE — 2 ELECTRIC LOCOS OFF AND WAITING — 2 ELECTRIC LOCOS →

IN GREATER MANCHESTER AREA — 2 ELECTRIC LOCOS OFF AND WAITING — BACK TO I DIESEL → — DESTINATION

Above: This included a table showing the many changes of locomotives from diesel to electric to diesel and also for banking purposes.

Below: British Railways in 1979 issued a booklet to explain the need for complete closure of the Woodhead route.

Trans-Pennine Routes "The Facts"

TOTAL CAPACITY 360 TRAINS

REQUIREMENT 154

A westbound (down) coal train passes Dunford Bridge station in 1978. However the line was closed to all traffic in July 1981. It cannot be said that the Woodhead route had been a success in all directions. Trains may have been accelerated but the load of a coal train had fallen from sixty-three 13-ton wagons with steam to only forty-eight with electrics.

23. Worsborough Bank.

The Manchester, Sheffield & Lincolnshire Railway opened the freight branch from Aldam junction to West Silkstone junction in 1882 which was to become an important freight route from Wath marshalling yard to Lancashire via the Woodhead tunnel. The purpose of the new line was to provide a route which avoided the difficult and congested journey through Barnsley for coal trains. However to achieve this necessitated the provision of a gradient of 1 in 40 for over two mile of the double track line.

This involved the coal trains having to be banked up the incline. As this was a difficult task the LNER in 1925 built the mammoth 6 cylinder Class U1 2-8-8-2 Beyer Garratt locomotive. This machine which was built by Beyer Peacock & Co. weighed 178 tons and needed a 7 foot diameter boiler to power it.

Coal trains weighing 850 tons would have a 2-8-0 locomotive at each end of the train until a stop was made at Wentworth at the foot of the gradient to attach the Garratt which would push the train to the summit at West Silkstone junction. Here it would detach itself from the train and return light to Wentworth.

The line was electrified in 1952 resulting in the coal trains being handled by four electric locomotives making the Garratt redundant. However with the decline of the coal industry the line closed completely in 1981 after almost 100 years service.

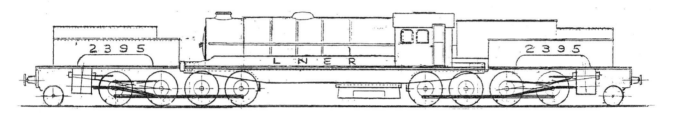

Gresley's LNER Class U1 2-8-0-0-8-2 Beyer Garratt locomotive
built 1925 for banking duties on the Worsborough incline of the Wath - Penistone line.

A pair of Class 76 EM1 electric locomotives descend Worsborough bank with coal empties off the Woodhead line in 1976. Swaithe viaduct in the background carries the former Midland Barnsey - Sheffield line.

24. The Stocksbridge Railway

This line ran from the Great Central main line at Deepcar to Stocksbridge. A passenger services was provided from 1877 which ran from the Samuel Fox steelworks to Deepcar. This was used almost exclusively by employees of the company and their children going to school. The service closed in 1931 but the line continued to be used for freight. Since the closure of the Woodhead route it has been operated as a siding from Woodburn junction.

South Yorkshire PTE however have long had aspirations to reopen the route to passengers. In the 1975 Land Use Transportation Study there was a proposal to use it as an electrified suburban railway with a single track underground loop line to serve Sheffield city centre. The plan was to have 15 minute frequent electric trains on each of four suburban routes from Stocksbridge, Barnsley, Mexborough / Doncaster and Kiverton Park / Mosborough. Interestingly the network was based upon ex Great Central routes to access the central loop line.

These rail proposals, which are shown on the attached diagram, were protected against development until early 1979 but the scheme was considered too expensive and plans subsequently emerged for a surface Supertram network..

The Transport Authority however would still like to make use of this railway and in it's 2009 Rail Strategy Plan document explored this possibility. In 2010 a feasibility study report concluded that the track was in good enough condition to operate a passenger service. Plans for a new station have been included in a new supermarket complex in Stocksbridge and further stations would be needed at Deepcar, Wharncliffe Side and Oughtibridge. Initial plans involve running a passenger service from Stocksbridge to the Supertram stop at Nunnery Square.

It will be interesting to see if these plans progress or perhaps a service could emerge as a Tram-Train operation linked to the Sheffield Supertram with through running into the centre of Sheffield .

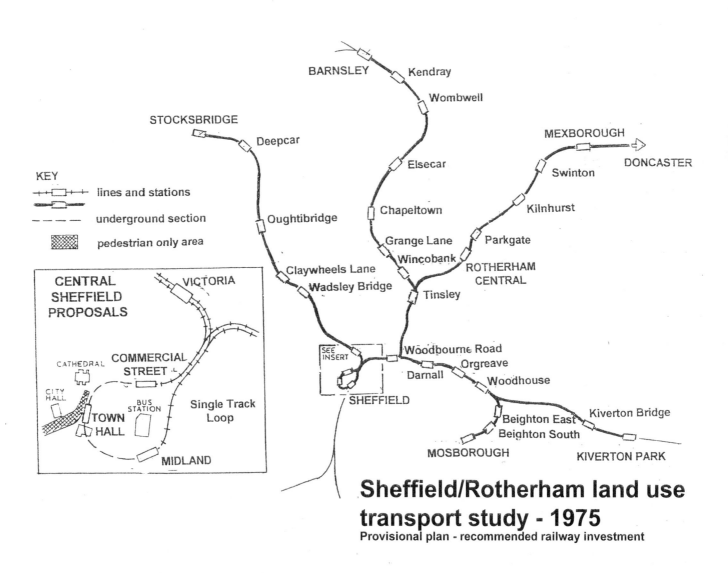

Sheffield/Rotherham land use transport study - 1975
Provisional plan - recommended railway investment

Wadsley Bridge station was closed to regular passenger services in 1959 but was retained for excursion and football trains. The name board proclaimed 'Wadsley Bridge - station for Sheffield Wednesday Football ground'. On match days trains were stopped specially until the service was diverted via Barnsley after which the station was served by occasional special trains up to the 1990's. This view is of the station in 1965 looking towards Sheffield with - unusually - an EE type 3 diesel heading towards Manchester. Photo: Stations UK

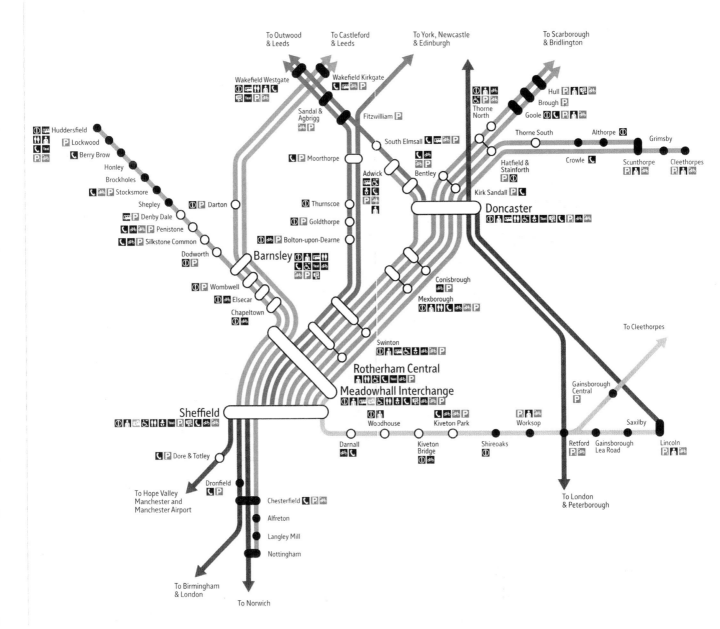

25. Hull & Barnsley Railway

This railway was incorporated in 1880 and opened a route from Hull to Cudworth in 1885. It's purpose was to carry coal from the South Yorkshire pits to the company's own dock at Hull for export. Despite it's name the company never reached Barnsley but terminated at a single platform which was part of the Midland station at Cudworth. A passenger service was operated from 1885 along with a branch service to Wath which started in 1902. Additionally an express service ran between Hull and Sheffield via Cudworth from 1905 until 1917 using running powers over the Midland. Most of the companies locomotives were mineral engines except for five 4-4-0 machines built in 1910 for the Sheffield express trains.

The Hull & Barnsley merged with it's competitor the North Easter Railway just prior to the groupings after which the route was progressively run down. The passenger service on the Wath branch closed in 1929 followed by services on the main line between South Howden and Cudworth in 1932. The line survived as a through route for freight until 1959.

Hull and Sheffield express service April 1910. This gave a respectable journey time of about 2 hours.

Some stops were made at Hull suburban stations and passengers changed at Cudworth for Barnsley. In addition a local service for intermediate stations was run between Hull and Cudworth until 1932. Local Hull to South Howden trains survived until 1955.

HULL & BARNSLEY HULL - SHEFFIELD EXPRESS SERVICE: 1910

UP				DOWN			
Hull Canon St.	09.40	15.00	17.00	Sheffield Midland	14.03	18.58	20.28
Howden	10.24	15.44	17.52	*Barnsley Court House*	*14.05*	*18.03*	*20.44*
Cudworth	11.10	16.33	18.20	Cudworth	14.35	19.29	20.58
Barnsley Court House	*11.25*	*17.08*	*20.25*	Howden	15.24	20.23	21.37
Sheffield Midland	11.45	17.03	18.55	Hull Canon St.	16.10	21.18	22.20

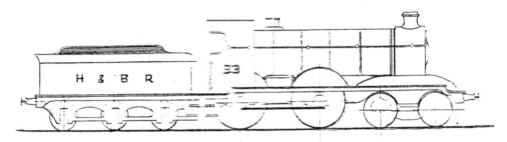

Hull & Barnsley Railway 4-4-0 passenger locomotive.
built 1910 by Kitson and Co. for Hull - Sheffield express service.

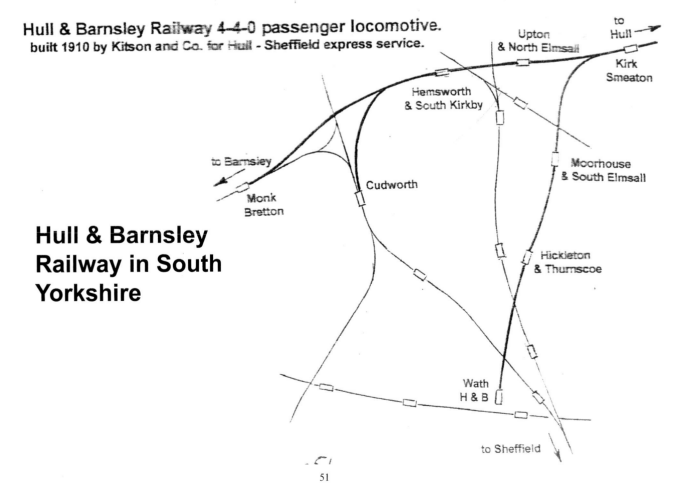

Hull & Barnsley Railway in South Yorkshire

26. The South Yorkshireman.

This was inaugurated by British Railways in 1948 as a name for a train of the existing service between Bradford and London via the Great Central main line. It left Bradford Exchange at 10.00 for Huddersfield then via Penistone to Sheffield Victoria before travelling express to London Marylebone where it was due to arrive at 15.10 with a return at 16.50 to be back in Bradford at 22.20.

Following withdrawal of this train in 1960 British Railways came under pressure from local communities to run a replacement train. In 1959 BR provided a Halifax to St. Pancras train routed via Thornhill junction and Royston. This was then altered to run into Huddersfield where it reversed before continuing through Mirfield then via Horbury West junction and Barnsley. In 1961 there was an even more extraordinary routing with the train leaving Halifax at 08.50 calling at Huddersfield at 09.10, Penistone 9.34 before using the closed Silkestone line to call Barnsley 9.51 and Sheffield Midland at 10.23 on route to St. Pancras.

However these services were short lived and the longer term solution was to run a through train from Halifax which departed at 8.30 and after reversal at Huddersfield and Wakefield Kirkgate was attached to a train from Leeds at Wakefield Westgate to arrive \ London \kings Cross at 13.05. The return train left Kings Cross at 19.00 running via Wakefield, Huddersfield and Halifax to terminate at Bradford Exchange at 23.19 These trains ceased to run with the arrival of the High Speed trains in 1978 when trains could no longer be divided into separate portions.

In 2000 Midland Main Line introduced a London St. Pancras to Barnsley service using DMU's which ran until 2007. Grand Central Railway Company revive a London direct service from Bradford in 2010 with three trains each way between Bradford Interchange (New name for the old Exchange station following the opening of an adjacent travel interchange in 1973) and London Kings Cross. The trains call at Halifax, Brighouse, Wakefield Kirkgate, Pontefract and Doncaster on route.

In 2009 Alliance Rail proposed another open access service of four trains per day from Huddersfield - Penistone - Barnsley - Sheffield - Retford to London Kings Cross. Whether this service will ever materialise is questionable.

Official launch of 'The South Yorkshireman' at Bradford Exchange station in 1948. This was the first named train introduced by British Railways. Ex-LMS Class 5 locomotive No 5101 carries the temporary prefix M for London Midland and shed plate 25A from Wakefield (Belle Vue) depot. One wonders why a Wakefield engine came to be selected for a Low Moor working. Picture: Transport Treasury.

27. The Bradford Connection

There was a long history of through running of services from Bradford to the Huddersfield area and Sheffield. Apart from 'The South Yorkshireman' a pre war named train was the LMS 'The Yorkshireman' which ran from Bradford Exchange express to Sheffield and then London St. Pancras. This was routed via the Spen Valley, Thornhill junction and Royston.

The LYR ran an intensive local service from Bradford Exchange, via both Halifax and the Spen Valley, through Huddersfield to Penistone and Clayton West. This was perpetuated by the LMS and also BR. When DMU's were introduced in 1959 the same pattern of services was operated until withdrawal in 1965.

When passenger services was restored between Bradford and Huddersfield in 2000 it was not possible to resume through running because track reductions and the massive increase in trans-pennine expresses reduced capacity which precluded the locals crossing over to access the Penistone line.

Huddersfield - Bradford.

BR standard 4-6-0 no. 73124 in grimy condition arrives at Huddersfield in 1964 with a parcel train from Leeds. It can be seen that this is on the through line which was to become the new platform 1 in 1990 when the new bay platform 2 was created. The platform face was moved up to the through track to enable the stepped bay platform to be provided. Picture D.K. Jones.

Ex Lancashire & Yorkshire Railway 2-4-2 Tank number 50807 at Hudderfield station platform 6 in 1952 with a local train for Bradford. Many of these trains ran through to the Penistone line rather than using the bay platforms. Note the water column on the platform for refreshing steam trains. Photo: Stephenson Locomotive Society.

The terminus Bradford Exchange station in the 1930's. Most trains for Penistone and Clayton West started from here as through services as did the London Marylebone trains. The station was jointly owned by the LYR and GNR. With the opening of the new Interchange station in 1973 the tracks were cut back to the near side of the bridge shown. Photo: Stations UK.

28. Huddersfield/Penistone and Sheffield Rail Users Association

Formed in 1981 to save the line from closure it opposed plans to withdraw passenger services on the line. The Association has gone from strength to strength in promoting and campaigning for improvements to services and membership is open to all users either regular or occasional. The Association campaigns for reliable and punctual services and wishes to see more modern trains, more double track and a half hourly service.

29. The Penistone Line Partnership

One of the first partnerships set up after the launch in 2004 of the Department of Transport's Commumity Rail Strategy. The Penistone Line Partnership was one of the first set up with the aim of breathing new life into local lines through community involvement. The Partnership has made great efforts to promote the railway including guided walks linked to train times and 'Real Ale' music trains.

30. The Denby Dale Pie

The world famous giant Denby Dale Pie grew to become a major event which attracted crowds from a wide area many of which came by train to Denby Dale station. The pie was first baked and eaten in 1788 to celebrate George III recovering his senses. This was repeated in 1815 to rejoice the defeat of Napoleon at Waterloo and in 1846 for the repeal of the Corn laws. Further circular pies followed in 1887 and 1896 while 1928 saw the first rectangular pie measuring 16 feet by 5 feet and weighing 4 tons. A further pie followed in 1964 for which 10 extra trains were operated.

The biggest pie of all was baked in 1988 and after a fun day event was cut into fifty thousand portions. West Yorkshire PTE promoted train travel as a means of reaching Denby Dale with an improved train services. However as the line through Denby Dale had been reduced to single track in 1969, there was a limit on track capacity although an augmented service was operated..

Denby Dale: A 3 car class 101 DMU leaves the single platform Denby Dale station for Sheffield in 1979. It can be seen that the station and track have been heavily rationalised - a feature that was to limit the trains which could be run for the 1988 Denby Dale pie event.

31. The Kirklees Light Railway.

This is a 4 mile long narrow gauge tourist railway which runs along the track bed of the former British Railways Clayton West branch line. The first section from Clayton West was opened in 1991 with the line later extended through Skelmanthorpe to a new Shelley terminal station at the end of the branch near Clayton West junction. Despite the tourist line being only half a mile away from Shepley station there is little effort to promote the Penistone line as a means of reaching the narrow gauge railway. The Kirklees Light Railway leaflet invites travellers arriving by train to catch a bus from either Shepley or Denby Dale stations which is hardly a practical proposition. A dedicated publicised footpath between Shepley and Shelley stations is required.

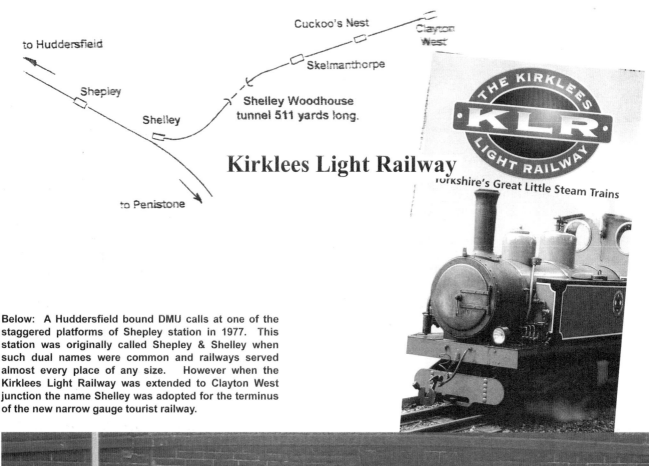

Kirklees Light Railway

Below: A Huddersfield bound DMU calls at one of the staggered platforms of Shepley station in 1977. This station was originally called Shepley & Shelley when such dual names were common and railways served almost every place of any size. However when the Kirklees Light Railway was extended to Clayton West junction the name Shelley was adopted for the terminus of the new narrow gauge tourist railway.

32. Elsecar Heritage Museum & Railway.

The Museum is based upon the former Wentworth Estate ironworks and colliery workshops of Earl Fitzwilliam which were purchased by Barnsley Council in 1988. This includes the Elsecar Steam Railway which operates a preserved tourist railway on part of the former track of the Elsecar branch of the South Yorkshire Railway opened in 1850. The line ceased to be used from 1984 following the closure of Cortonwood colliery.

An Easter Egg Special train leaves Rockingham station for the one mile trip to Hemmingfield on the Elsecar Heritage Centre railway in 2010. The railway has plans to extend the line a further mile to a new terminus at Cortonwood

33. South Yorkshire Railway.

This railway was originally formed as the Hallamshire Railway Society in 1974 as a locomotive owners group. With help from Sheffield City Council a home was eventually found at Meadow Hall at the southern end of the ex GCR Blackburn Valley line. The society then formed a new company the South Yorkshire Railway Co. Ltd. taking the name of the original company who opened the line.

The original railway was closed to passenger traffic in 1953 but continued to be used as a through route for freight until 1966 and as a freight siding until 1987.

The new company intended to reopen the Meadow Hall to Chapeltown section of the old ex GCR route as an heritage railway.

Little progress has been made in developing a working railway but the site was advertised as a railway centre with exhibits of over 40 locomotives including steam engines and rolling stock. The site had much potential with a great location next to the Meadowhall Interchange and Shopping Centre. However in 2004 the project folded and parts of the line were converted into a cycle track. A project with great potential which unfortunately did not materialise.

South Yorkshire Railway

A Railway Renaissance

South Yorkshire Railway

Barrow Road Sidings
Meadow Hall
Sheffield 9

34. Sheffield Supertram

The Royal Assent for construction of the first Supertram lines to Middlewood and Halfway was given on 27th. October 1988 with approval for the Don Valley and Meadowhall line following a year later on 21st. December 1989. However the first line to be opened was to Meadowhall on 21st. March 1994 with completion of the network a year later.

The Meadowhall line includes the Nunnery depot and runs from Sheffield city centre up the Don Valley along side the former ex Great Central line from Sheffield Victoria which is still open as a single track freight line. There are two stations to serve the Meadowhall shopping centre the first is called Meadowhall South / Tinsley where the tram route veers left and uses the trackbed of the former Sheffield Victoria to Barnsley line until reaching the present Sheffield - Rotherham line where it turns sharply left again to run parallel to the railway into Meadowhall interchange.

The Tram - Train trial for Rotherham proposes to connect to the Sheffield Supertram. The original plans for this were to use the Penistone line with diesel trams to Sheffield station but with phase 2 connected to the Sheffield tram route instead. This was switched in 2009 to the Rotherham route using all electric vehicles. Trams would run from Sheffield city centre on the existing tram route to South Meadowhall / Tinsley where a new junction would be provided to connect to the adjacent freight line to Rotherham Central before continuing to a new terminus at Parkgate Shopping centre.

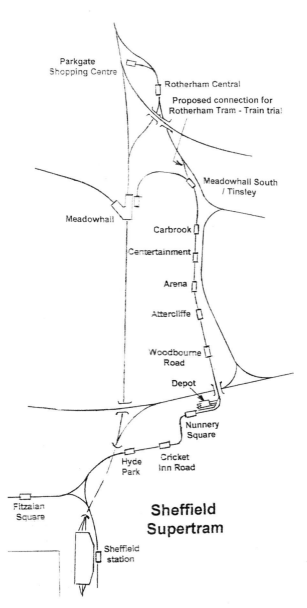

Sheffield Supertram

A Meadowhall - Sheffield City centre Supertram calls at the Meadowhall South/Tinsley stop in 1994. It is here that a connection to the parallel ex-GCR line is proposed for the Tram - Train trial to run to Rotherham. The now demolished cooling towers of Tinsley power station can be seen in the background.

35. Railway Walks

South Yorkshire as we have seen had numerous duplicate railways which have now been mostly closed. However an important legacy is that some of the key routes have survived as footpaths. Of particular interest is the ex Great Central main line from Penistone to Dunford Bridge and walkers can also enjoy the old freight line from Wath to Silkstone taking in the old Worsborough incline where freight trains once struggled to propel heavy freights across the pennines. These have become part of the Trans pennine trail, incorporating also parts of the Midland line and ex GC Barnsley to Doncaster trackbed.

Top right: A 2010 view of the buildings and pit head of Barnsley Main Colliery which has been preserved as a reminder of Barnsley's coalfield heritage.

Left: The Worsborough bank footpath looking towards Wath in 2010. Overhead is Swaith viaduct which carries the existing Barnsley to Sheffield railway across the vale.   Those of middle age and less can have no idea of the noise, steam and smoke that this idyll once witnessed.

Closed railways converted to footpaths and cycleways.

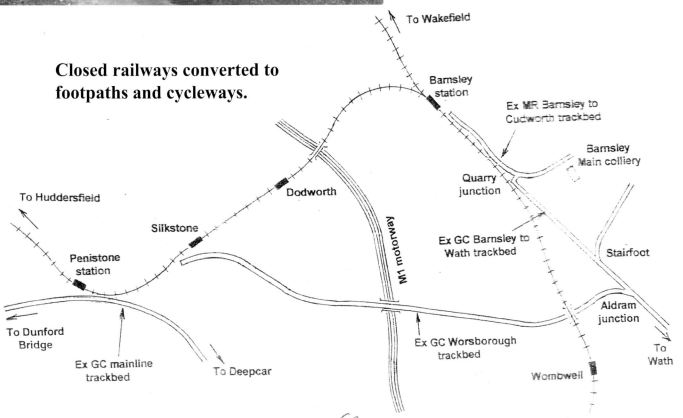

36 Stations

Station	No. platforms	Step free access	Car park Spaces	Number of daily trains	Annual patronage
Huddersfield	6	Yes	150	435	3,774,000
Lockwood	1	Yes	14	36	33,282
Berry Brow	1	Yes	0	36	27,581
Honley	1	No	7	36	49,183
Brockholes	1	Yes	0	36	42,893
Stocksmoor	2	Yes	6	36	22,109
Shepley	2	No	0	36	57,842
Denby Dale	1	Yes	9	36	119,952
Penistone	2	Yes	15	36	100,633
Silkstone	1	Yes	5	36	24,800
Dodworth	1	Yes	10	36	25,572
Barnsley	2	Yes	82	132	1,080,487
Wombwell	2	Yes	72	71	136,050
Elsecar	2	Yes	0	45	102,591
Chapeltown	2	Yes	0	71	194,747
Meadowhall	4	Yes	330	298	1,496,729
Sheffield	9	Yes	678	544	8,177,000

A Class 144 unit leaves the single platform Lockwood station for Sheffield in a snowstorm in 2010. The route is a lifeline for local communities during heavy snow falls when roads are often impassable. This part of the route was singled in 1989 but may need to be restored to double track in the future. The station is located next to the David Brown engineering works and in the pre- Beeching years well over 100 passengers would alight or join some of the trains.

A view of the original Berry Brow station looking south in 1968 two years after closure. Both platforms were situated in a steep narrow cutting resulting in cramped facilities. A single-platformed halt built on the up trackbed was opened in 1989 after the singling of the line. Picture: Stations UK.

Brockholes station in 1955 looking north with Fowler Class 4 tank No. 42310 heading a train for Penistone. The station has full facilities including a footbridge. Picture: Stations UK.

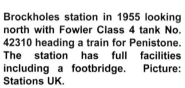

Brockholes in 2009 with a Class 150 unit approaching from Sheffield. The station has been reduced to a single platform although the up buildings and platform survive out of railway use. The line traverses the Pennine foothills and is a useful stabdby when weather forces the closure of roads.

A Hudderfield to Sheffield train calls at Stocksmoor station in 1988. Apart from the conversion to an unmanned halt, the station has changed little over the years. Proposals in the 1980's would have singled the line from Clayton West Junction to Huddersfield but in the end the Shepley to Stocksmoor stretch was retained as double track.

A view of Denby Dale station looking south in 1968, the year before the track was singled with the platform on the right being abandoned and the remainder of the station being left as a very basic unmanned halt.

A Class 101 DMU forms a train for Sheffield at the newly reopened station at Silkstone Common in 1985. The original station here closed in 1959.

A Class 142 unit calls at the reopened Dodworth station after its reduction to a single platform in 1989; thirty years after the closure of the original station in 1959.

A view looking towards Barnsley of two DMU's crossing at Wombwell station in 1977.

A Class 111 unit bound for Leeds leaves Elsecar station in 1984.

The 12.15 Sheffield Midland to Barnsley Court House train calls at Chapeltown Midland station in 1955 headed by Royston 2-4-2T No. 50650 which was standing in for the usual LMS 2-6-2T. Photo: Initial Photographics.

In contrast to the view above, a Sheffield-bound dmu calls at the newly opened Chapeltown station which was situated two hundred yards towards Sheffield. The coal, iron and chemical traffic which had made the older location so profitable had long evaporated by 1982 when the photograph was taken.

Meadowhall station which opened in 1990 to serve a new shopping centre. The new station has four platforms, extensive car parking, a bus station and, from 1994, a Supertram connection. Here a Class 101 unit forms a service to Leeds.

A Meadowhall scene of 2010: a Class 153 unit forms a Northern train for Doncaster and Adwick at platform 2 and passes a Class 170 unit working a Trans-Pennine express from Cleethorpes to Manchester Piccadilly in Platform 1.

A Sheffield to Leeds train passes through Brightside station in 1988. Only a few trains stopped at the station which was closed in 1995. The opening of Meadowhall in 1990 had in any case made it redundant.

A Class 144 unit passes Attercliffe Road station in 1988. Although used by office workers, few trains stopped at the station and it was closed in 1995 although the platforms have been left in place.

37. The future?

Clearly this is a magnificent line but how will it develop next? The shelving of the Tram - Train trial has left the line in a vacuum with overcrowded trains but no plans to improve matters. Most of the route has only a basic hourly service which is no longer good enough in an age of mobility. As the line has so much heavy engineering which is expensive to maintain the maximum advantage should be taken of this to provide the best possible service.

The greatest need is a half hourly service. To achieve this an additional passing loop will probably need to be provided at Lockwood and possibly the Penistone loop lengthened. Currently the service is operated very efficiently by three train units. To increase the frequency two obvious options are possible. The first is to employ two extra units to run between Huddersfield and Barnsley while the second would use three extra trains to provide the full service to Sheffield. The extra trains could run non stop between Barnsley and Meadowhall improving journey times between the two main centres of Huddersfield and Sheffield while some of the rural more lightly used stations could become tram type request stops.

Some station facilities are below standard. Honley and Shepley do not have step free access and this needs to be rectified. In West Yorkshire there is a chronic shortage of car parking at stations. Searches should be made for sites for more car parking spaces particularly at Honley and Denby Dale.

Given these improvements there is no reason why the line should not go from strength to strength and develop as an important commuter route and be enjoyed as one of Yorkshire's most scenic railways through the beautiful pennine countryside.

38. Acknowledgements

Thanks are due to the many people who have helped me compile this book particularly library staff who have assisted in the search through old documents and ordnance survey maps and Richard Fieldhouse the Chairman of the Huddersfield, Penistone & Sheffield Rail Users Association. Also appreciated is the help of photographers who have allowed the publication of their photographs. Unaccredited photographs are either by myself or from my collection of old pictures; the sources of which are unknown.

Further reading:

Along the Penistone Line, Peter Thomas.
The Huddersfield & Sheffield junction Railway, Martin Bairstow.
A Regional History of the Railways of Great Britain. Volume 8 - South & West Yorkshire, David Joy.
Rail Centres - Sheffield, Stephen R Batty.

Although this book has concentrated on passenger activities in South Yorkshire, the reality is that until the early 1970's goods and mineral traffic was the dominant element in railway operations and for every passenger train there were several dozen goods workings. A reminder of this former activity is given by Mexborough-based Austerity 2-8-0 77138 (later 90587) at West Silkstone junction in 1950. The overhead gantries have already been erected as part of the Wath - Manchester electrification.. Photo: BWLB / Initial Photographics.

39. Appendix
1 - Railway companies and organisations.

BR (ER)   - British Railways Eastern Region.
BR (NER)   - British Railways North Eastern Region.
BR (LMR)   - British Railways London Midland Region
LNER   - London & North Eastern Railway
GCR   - Great Central Railway
MSL   - Manchester, Sheffield & Lincolnshire Railway
SAM   - Sheffield, Ashton-under-Lyne & Manchester Railway
SYR   - South Yorkshire Railway
NER (HBR)   - North Eastern Railway (ex Hull & Barnsley Railway)
LMS   - London Midland & Scottish Railway
Mid.   - Midland Railway
SR   - Sheffield & Rotherham Railway
NM   - North Midland Railway
LYR   - Lancashire & Yorkshire Railway
SRBWHG   - Sheffield, Rotherham. Barnsley Wakefield, Huddersfield & Goole Railway
HSJ   - Huddersfield & Sheffield Junction Railway.
TUCC   - Transport Users Consultative Committee.
RDS   - Railway Development Society (Yorkshire branch)
HPSRUA   - Huddersfield, Penistone, Sheffield Rail Users Association.
WYPTA and SYPTA - West and South Yorkshire Passenger Transport Authorities.

Note: Penistone - Barnsley - Sheffield was always part of BR Eastern Region. Leeds - Huddersfield to near Penistone part of BR London Midland Region until transferred to the North Eastern Region in 1956. North Eastern Region absorbed into Eastern Region of BR in 1967.

2. Engine Sheds

Ex - LNER steam		Ex - LMS steam		BR - DMU depots	
Sheffield Neepsend	closed 1943	Sheffield Grimesthorpe (Brightside) closed 1961		Bradford Hammerton Street (HS) 1961-84	
Sheffield Darnall	closed 1963	Sheffield Millhouses closed 1962		Sheffield Darnall (DA) 1964 - 1987	
Mexborough	closed 1964	Rotherham Canklow closed 1965		Leeds Neville Hill (NH)	
Barnsley	closed 1960	Royston closed 1967			
Cudworth (ex HBR) closed 1951		Huddersfield Hillhouse closed 1967			
		Bradford Low Moor closed 1967			

Following the closure of the DMU (Diesel Multiple Unit) depot at Sheffield Darnall (DA) the stabling and servicing of units was performed at Sheffield station (SM)   West & South Yorkshire DMU's are today maintained at Leeds Neville Hill depot (NH).

Diesel locomotive depot
Tinsley (TI)   1965 - 1998
Electric locomotive depot.
Wath (WH)   1952 - 1981

Sheffield Supertram.

The tram depot for the Sheffield Supertram network is located at Nunnery. Here a Meadowhall to Sheffield bound tram passes the depot in 2010.

Steam locomotive sheds - ex LNER.

A general view of Sheffield Darnall in 1949. The depot, which opened in 1943 as a replacement for Neepsend shed, provided engines for Sheffield Victoria and Bernard Road together with the trip workings for the area. Electrification made little difference to the shed's allocation which remained static throughout the fifties at 22 passenger engines and 74 goods. Photo: BWLB / Initial Photographics.

A view of Mexborough shed in 1949. Mexborough was the largest shed on the ex Great Central and provided motive power for services over the Manchester - Cleethorpes axis of the system. Although many of its turns to Manchester were eliminated by the Wath - Manchester electrification of 1954, Mexborough lost only 24 of its 119 engines. A measure of the work encompassed by the depot is given by the fact that only 6 of the 119 locomotives allocated were passenger engines. Photo: Initial Photographics / BWLB.

A view of Barnsley GC shed and the curious single platformed Exchange station. looking north in 1959. Its allocation of around forty engines - half of which were 2-8-0's for trip workings - remained static until 1960 when the depot's work was taken over by Mexborough. Closure of the shed allowed a second platform to be added to the station. Picture: Transport Treasury.

Steam locomotive sheds - ex LMS.

The principal LMS passenger depot at Sheffield was Millhouses Loco which provided engines for services based on Sheffield Midland.

2P 4-4-0 411 is seen on Sheffield Millhouses shed in 1938. Photo: RJB / Initial Photographics.

Ex Midland Railway 0-6-0 Class 3F locomotive number 3731 at Sheffield Brightside shed in 1951. The official name of this shed was Sheffield Grimesthorpe but it was generally referred to as Brightside. Photo: RJB/ Initial Photographics.

A view of Canklow locomotive depot in 1949. This shed provided locomotives for freight duties over the ex LMS lines in the Rotherham area. Photo: Initial Photographics / BWLB.

Other depots and locomotives.

Gresley's mammoth Garret banking locomotive number 69999 at it's home shed Mexborough in early BR days before being made redundant by electrification. It was the only locomotive to be fitted with respirators and was so powerful that it would buckle the brakevan floors of trains being banked. Picture Transport Treasury.

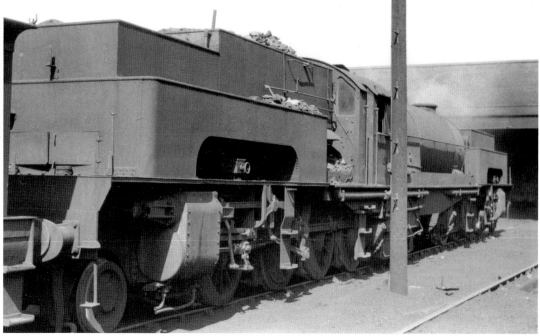

One advantage of electrification was that no running sheds were needed and when not in use, electric engines were simply parked on a siding; engines being picked up when needed for a train. Maintenance was carried out at Reddish, Wath and, for a short time, Darnall electric depots. A row of Electric locomotives waiting work is seen at Wath in 1968. Number 26029 is the nearest. Photo RCTS

The LMS shed for the Barnsley area was Royston located near Cudworth on the Midland main line. With an allocation of about 60 locomotives - one third of which were 8F 2-8-0's - the shed played an important role in providing engines for trip workings to the many collieries in the area and for trains to and from the L&Y system at Wakefield. The shed remained open until the early 1970's. Picture: D.K. Jones.

Chronology of Huddersfield - Penistone - Barnsley - Sheffield Passenger Railways.

Date	Railway	Section of line
31.10.1838	SR / Mid	Sheffield Wicker - Rotherham Westgate opened
30.6.1840	NMR / Mid	Rotherham - Leeds (Midland main line) opened
14.7.1845	SAM / GC	Sheffield Bridgehouse - Dunford Bridge (Great Central) main line opened
1.1.1850	SRBWHG/ LYR	Horbury Jcn. - Barnsley Exchange opened
1.7.1850	HSJ / LYR	Huddersfield - Penistone Brockholes - Holmfirth opened
1.7.1851	SYR / GC	Mexborough - Barnsley Exchange opened
15.9.1851	MSL	Sheffield Victoria station opened, Bridgehouses closed.
4.9.1854	SY / GC	Wincobank Blackburn Jcn. - Stairfoot Aldham Jcn. opened. Sheffield - Barnsley service introduced reversing at Wombwell.
1.12.1859	MSL / GC	Penistone - Barnsley opened
1.8.1864	SY / GC	Woodburn Jcn. - Meadow Hall opened. Permitted Barnsley services to run to Sheffield Victoria.
5.7.1869	LYR	Lockwood Meltham Jcn. - Meltham opened
1.2.1870	Mid	Tapton Jcn. (Chesterfield) - Grimesthorpe junction (between Sheffield and Rotherham) opened including Sheffield Midland station. Sheffield Wicker station closed.
1.5.1870	Mid	Cudworth S Jcn. - Barnsley Court House W Jcn. opened.
31.5.1870	MSL / GC	Quarry Jcn. - Court House W Jcn. opened.
23.8.1873		Opening of Barnsley Court House station.
1.9.1879	LYR	Shepley Jcn. - Clayton West opened
1.12.1879	MSL / GC	Wombwell Main Jcn. - New Oates Jcn. opened. Removed the need for reversal at Wombwell.
1.9.1882	MSL / GC	Stairfoot Old Oakes Jcn. - Nostell N Jcn. Stairfoot - Oakwell Jcn. opened.
1.7.1897	Mid	Wincobank station Jcn. - Barnsley Court House W Jcn opened..
11.9.1899	Mid	Monkspring Jcn. - Cudworth S Jcn. Opened.
1.1.1923	LNER / LMS	Grouping of Railways into four national companies served locally by LNER and LMS.
26.9.1927	LNER	Attercliffe station closed
22.9.1930	LNER	Barnsley Court House - Wakefield service via Nostell withdrawn and Staincross and Notton & Royston stations closed.
27.9.1937	LMS	Monk Bretton station closed
28.10.1940	LNER	Neepsend station closed
1.1.1948	BR	Nationalisation of railways
23.5.1949	BR (LMR)	Huddersfield - Meltham local service and Netherton, Healey House and Meltham stations closed.
29.10.1951	BR (ER)	Tinsley station closed.
7.12.1953	BR (ER)	Barnsley Court House - Sheffield Victoria local service and Dovecliffe, Birdwell & Hoyland Common, Chapeltown Central, Ecclesfield East, Grange Lane and Meadow Hall stations closed.
3.6.1954	BR (ER)	Completion of Sheffield / Wath - Manchester electrification.
2.5.1955	BR (ER)	Wortley station closed
19.9.1955	BR (ER)	Holmes station closed
2.4.1956	BR (ER)	Wincobank station closed
3.4.1956	BR (ER)	Broughton Lane station closed.
16.9.1957	BR (ER)	Stairfoot for Ardsley station closed.
3.3.1958	BR (NER)	Leeds City - Barnsley Exchange DMU service via Wakefield Kirkgate introduced.
9.6.1958	BR (NER)	Cudworth - Barnsley Court House closed
5.1.1959	BR (ER)	Sheffield Midland - York DMU's introduced Sheffield Midland - Barnsley Court House DMU's introduced.
15.6.1959	BR (ER)	Sheffield Victoria - Penistone local service and stations at Wadsley Bridge, Oughty Bridge and Deepcar closed.
29.6.1959	BR (ER)	Penistone - Doncaster local service and Silkstone, Dodworth, Summer Lane, Wombwell Central and Wath Central stations closed.
2.11.1959	BR (NER)	Holmfirth branch and Thongs Bridge and Holmfirth stations closed Wentworth station closed. DMU's introduced Bradford Exchange - Huddersfield - Penistone / Clayton West.

19.4.1960	BR (ER)	New connection at Quarry junction opened resulting in closure of Barnsley Court House station and introduction of new Leeds City - Barnsley Exchange - Sheffield DMU service.
1961 - 1966	BR (NER)	Intermediate stations Huddersfield - Penistone destaffed and Paytrains introduced followed later by stations on Leeds - Barnsley - Sheffield line.
13.9.1965	BR (NER)	Crigglestone and Haigh stations closed.
4.7.1966	BR (NER)	Berry Brow station closed.
5.9.1966	BR (ER)	Rotherham Central Station closed.
6.11.1967	BR (ER)	Ecclesfield West station closed
1.1.1968	BR (ER)	Leeds City - Barnsley service via Cudworth withdrawn and Cudworth and Wath North stations closed.
24.11.1969	BR (ER)	Clayton West junction to Penistone section reduced to single track.
5.1.1970	BR (ER)	Manchester - Sheffield Victoria electric passenger service withdrawn. New diesel service Huddersfield to Sheffield Midland via Penistone with reversal at Woodburn Jcn. Sheffield Victoria station closed.
17.7.1981	BR (ER) & (LMR)	Penistone - Hadfield (Woodhead line) closed to all traffic.
24.1.1983	BR (ER)	Skelmanthorpe and Clayton West stations and branch line closed. Huddersfield to Sheffield trains re-routed to run via Barnsley. Penistone - Deepcar line closed, Deepcar - Nunnery retained for freight.
28.11.1984	BR (ER)	Silkstone Common station opened
11.5.1987	BR (ER)	Rotherham Central and Holmes chord line opened.
3.10.1988	BR (ER)	Rotherham Masborough station closed.
15.5.1989	BR (ER)	Dodworth station opened.
9.10.1989	BR (ER)	Berry Brow station opened. Springwood junction - Stocksmoor section reduced to single track.
8.9.1990	BR (ER)	Meadowhall station opened.
28.1.1995	BR (ER)	Brightside and Attercliffe Road stations closed.

Class 45 diesel locomotive 45134 with a Kings Cross to York special enters Huddersfield over the Longroyd bridge having travelled via Retford, Sheffield and Penistone in 20th December 1986. Picture: Gavin Morrison.

4. The Huddersfield, Penistone, Sheffield Rail Users Association.
The Fight to save the Penistone line 1963-1988

1963 - The Reshaping of British Railways report by BR pronounced the closure of passenger services and stations Huddersfield - Clayton West / Penistone. There were 87 official objectors to the closure but several had petitions attached with a total of 561 signatures.

1964 - BR commenced a programme of closure of goods yards and associated signal boxes. TUCC closure procedure for passenger services and stations commenced with a public hearing at Huddersfield on 10th. September 1964.

1965 - The freight branches to Meltham and Holmfirth were closed.

1966 - The Minister of Transport, Mrs. Barbara Castle MP, refused consent to closure on 22nd. April 1966. BR responded by closing Berry Brow station on 2nd. July 1966 and fully de-staffed all intermediate stations except Penistone from the 9th. October 1966. Note: Pay Trains had been introduced on Penistone line services from the Autumn of 1961.

1967 - Train service reduced to virtually peak hours only from 5th. June 1967.

1968 - Transport Act established Transport Authorities in Metropolitan areas with powers to fund local public transport.

1969 - BR singled the line between Clayton West Junction and Penistone from 24th. November 1969.

1970 - The Manchester to Sheffield Victoria via Penistone electric passenger service closed and replaced by Huddersfield - Sheffield DMU's running non stop from Penistone to Sheffield Midland with a reversal at Nunnery from 5th. January 1970.

1974 - South and West Yorkshire Passenger Transport Authorities formed in April 1974 with powers to financially support the local rail services that they wish to keep using Section 20 of the 1968 Transport Act. .

1977 - WYPTA agree to financially support Huddersfield to Denby Dale but not the service to Clayton West. SYPTA agree to financially support the service from Sheffield to Barnsley and Darton but not the service from Sheffield to Penistone.

1980 - Proposal to divert service via Barnsley but inconclusive negotiations resulted in closure process starting all over again. BR issued a Section 56 (7) formal closure notice under the 1962 Transport Act on 24th. September for Sheffield Nunnery to Denby Dale (exclusive) and Clayton West Junction to Clayton West.

1981 - The RDS arranged a public meeting in Huddersfield on 21st. March to set up HPSRUA to oppose the closures. Members of the new Association presented evidence to the TUCC closure hearings at Huddersfield and Sheffield.

1982 - The Secretary of State for Transport agreed in August 1982 to the closures but with a delay to the Penistone service until May 1983 to allow negotiations to continue on a diverted service via Barnsley.

1983 - Clayton West branch closed on 22nd. January. The direct line from Sheffield to Penistone closed on 14th. May 1983 and was replaced by a diverted 12 months experimental service via Barnsley, funded under the Speller Amendment (Section 56A), on the 16th. May 1983. On 8th. September 1983 BR issued a Section 56 (7) closure notice for Denby Dale to Huddersfield.

1984 - SYPTA agreed full Section 20 support for Sheffield - Penistone from 16th. May 1984. At the same time WYPTA withdraws Section 20 financial support for Huddersfield to Denby Dale services. HPSRUA organises public meetings to object to proposed closure. New station opened at Silkestone Common on 26th. November.

1985 - Numerous public meetings and lobbying of MP's and council's. HPSRUA presented strong case on hardship at TUCC closure hearings at Huddersfield on October 21st. and 22nd. and Stocksmoor on 2nd. November 1985.

1986 - HPSRUA invited to TUCC press conference on 12th. March 1986 and informed that the TUCC would be recommending opposition to closure on the grounds of severe hardship with HPSRUA evidence pivotal in the decision. This was followed up by lobbying of WYPTA.

1987 - WYPTA agreed to financial Section 20 support for the Huddersfield to Denby Dale trains from 5th. October 1987.

1988 - A much improved hourly weekday timetable introduced from 16th. May 1988 and a summer Sunday service from 22nd. May 1988.

The HPSRUA played a crucial role in saving Penistone line trains with members of the Association lobbying Governments, Transport Authorities, Councils, MP's and Railway Companies which they continue to do to this day..

Compiled by
Richard Fieldhouse, Chairman.

Low Moor 5MT 4-6-0 No. 45208 leaves Honley tunnel and passes under an ex LYR signal gantry before entering Honley station in 1959. Picture: Gavin Morrison.

5. Penistone line train services since 1850.

From Huddersfield, number of trains per day (one direction)

To:	HSJ 1850		LYR 1880		LNWR 1922		LMS 1938		BR (LMR) 1948	
	Wkd	Sun	Wkd	Sun	Wkd	Sun	Wkd	Sun	Wkd	Sun
Penistone	5	2	12	3	9	3	10	3	12	3
Holmfirth	6	2	10	3	17	3	17	3	6	0
Meltham			7	2	13	2	9	0	4	0
Clayton West			5	0	10	0	10	0	5	0
Barnsley				X		X		X		X
Sheffield		X		X		X		X		X

To:	BR (NER) 1960		BR (NER) 1970		BR (ER) 1984		NS 2000		NR 2010	
	Wkd	Sun	Wkd	Sun	Wkd	Sun	Wkd	Sun	Wkd	Sun
Penistone	15	4*	9	0	8	0	18	6	18	8
Holmfirth										
Meltham										
Clayton West	5	0	4	0						
Barnsley			8	0	7	0	18	6	18	8
Sheffield		X	8	0	7	0	18	6	18	8

X Change at Penistone   * no intermediate stops winter but 4 stops summer.   **NS** Northern Spirit
NR Northern Rail Ltd.

A Class 101 DMU arriving at Clayton West with the 12.10 ex Huddersfield in/1982. The signal box dates from 1878 and served the branch until being taken out of use in 1983. Picture: Gavin Morrison.

6. Penistone Line signal boxes from 1874.

Signalbox / location	Owner	Year	Closure	Remarks
Huddersfield no.1	LNWR	1886	1958	Replaced by power box
Huddersfield no.2	LNWR	1886	1958	
Huddersfield power box	BR (NER)	1958		Control area extended 1961 - 93
Springwood junction	LNWR	1886	1961	
Lockwood no.1	LYR	1874	1961	
Meltham junction	LYR	1874	1897	Replaced by Lockwood box no.2
Lockwood no.2	LYR	1897	1968	
Berry Brow	LYR	1874	1961	
Honley station	LYR	1874	1964	Replaced by larger box 1890
Brockholes junction	LYR	1874	1966	
Stocksmoor station	LYR	1874	1965	
Shepley station	LYR	1874	1965	
Clayton West junction	LYR	1879	1989	Replaced by larger box 1915
Denby Dale station	LYR	1874	1965	Replaced by larger box 1917
Penistone station	LYR	1874	1964?	
Penistone junction	MSL	1888	1998	Control transferred to Barnsley

Also signalboxes at Meltham (1896 - 1952), Thongs Bridge (1881 - 1961), Holmfirth (1882 - 1961), Skelmanthorpe (1879 - 1897), Clayton West (1878 - 1983).

The Penistone line continued to operate as a main line until the late 1960's, Here Jubilee Class 4-6-0 No. 45647 'Sturdee' crosses Penistone viaduct with the summer Poole - Bradford Exchange Saturdays only express in July 1966. Picture: Gavin Morrison.

Apart from the Austerity 2-8-0's which worked the coal traffic, BR Standards were rare sights on the Penistone line and were usually found only on enthusiasts specials, one of which brought Britannia class no. 70013 'Oliver Cromwell' to the line in 1967. It is seen bursting out of the tunnel at Lockwood station. Picture: Gavin Morrison.